The Savoy Cocktail Book

Must Have Books
503 Deerfield Place
Victoria, BC
V9B 6G5
Canada

ISBN: 9781773238104

Copyright 2021 – Must Have Books

All rights reserved in accordance with international law. No part of this book may be reproduced or transmitted in any form or by any means, electronic or mechanical, including photocopying, recording, or by any information storage or retrieval system, except in the case of excerpts by a reviewer who may quote brief passages in an article or review, without written permission from the publisher.

"If all be true that I do think,
There are five reasons why men drink,
Good wine, a friend, or being dry,
Or lest we should be by-and-by,
Or any other reason why."

Henry Aldrich (1647—1710).

The Savoy Cocktail Book

BEING in the main a complete compendium of the Cocktails, Rickeys, Daisies, Slings, Shrubs, Smashes, Fizzes, Juleps, Cobblers, Fixes, and other Drinks, known and vastly appreciated in this year of grace 1930, with sundry notes of amusement and interest concerning them, together with subtle Observations upon Wines and their special occasions. BEING in the particular an elucidation of the Manners and Customs of people of quality in a period of some equality.

The Cocktail Recipes in this Book have been compiled by
HARRY CRADDOCK
OF THE
SAVOY HOTEL
LONDON.

The Decorations are by Gilbert Rumbold.

Professor Jerry Thomas, the greatest Bartender of the Past, mixing his famous " Blue Blazer " at the Metropolitan Hotel, New York, in the " Roaring Fifties ".

THIS BOOK

IS

DEDICATED

TO

YOU

PREFACE.

MANY have been the books written about the proper way of partaking of wine. Paris, London and New York have given us many good little Cocktail Books.

But where, Oh, *where* is the book that gives the earnest student *all*? Every beautiful and perfect Wine, each with its own special and perfect occasion, and *every* Cocktail known? We searched, and found it not, so thought it as well to sit down and get it put together.

Presumption? Yes,—and we have been warned against it! Writers never get paid. Anyhow we're so rich we don't care if it costs us millions. A complete, and absolutely complete book on Drinks and Drinking, Cocktails and Wines, has simply *GOT* to be written. Nearly all the kind friends in the world are going to read it through—they may prevent it from being too dull.

FOREWORD.

IF everyone knew even a little about the absorbing subject of absorbing alcohol there would be even less Prohibition in the United States of America than there is now. The great mistake is that everyone knows either too little or too much. Those who know too little either do not admit their lack of knowledge and make an enemy of alcohol by abusing it, or are so terrified of it that they regard it as being something supernatural and satanic and utterly anathema. Those who know too much about it become intolerant of every form of liquid which does not happen to be the one concerning which they consider themselves to be expert.

Wine was created for the solace of man, as a slight compensation, we are told, for the creation of woman, who was merely created to keep him on the move and busy generally. In moments of stress and strain wine is man's greatest friend. Once, many years ago, a great and good man, somewhat my senior in age, made a very shrewd and important observation to me. We had been discussing the misfortunes of a mutual friend who

COCKTAILS

had been working so hard that he had forced himself into a state of brain-fever : a salient point in the case was that he imagined he could keep his brain clearer by eating and drinking extremely little, whereas this abstemiousness on his part had only succeeded in hastening his collapse.

" My boy," said my friend to me, " Let this be a solemn lesson to us all to eat as much good food, and drink as much good wine, as we possibly can, when and wherever the opportunity presents itself, no matter what it costs —or who pays for it."

A FEW HINTS FOR THE YOUNG MIXER.

1. Ice is nearly always an absolute essential for any Cocktail.

2. Never use the same ice twice.

3. Remember that the ingredients mix better in a shaker rather larger than is necessary to contain them.

4. Shake the shaker as hard as you can : don't just rock it : you are trying to wake it up, not send it to sleep !

5. If possible, ice your glasses before using them.

6. Drink your Cocktail as soon as possible. Harry Craddock was once asked what was the best way to drink a Cocktail : " *Quickly*," replied that great man, " while it's laughing at you ! "

CONTENTS

	Page
PREFACE	7
FOREWORD	8

PART I.

	Page
COCKTAILS : Historical Note	13
Cocktail recipes in alphabetical order	16
Prepared Cocktails for Bottling	182
Non-Alcoholic Cocktails	184
Cocktails suitable for a Prohibition Country	184
SOURS	186
TODDIES	186
FLIPS	187
EGG NOGGS	188
TOM COLLINS	189
SLINGS	190
SHRUBS	191
SANGAREES	192
HIGHBALLS	192
FIZZES	193
COOLERS	201
RICKEYS	203
DAISIES	204
FIXES	205

CONTENTS
Continued

					Page
JULEPS	..	..	..	..	..	206
SMASHES	..	..	..	>.	..	208
COBBLERS	..	..	..	..	..	209
FRAPPÉ	..	..	..	..	..	209
PUNCHES	..	..	..	..	..	210
CUPS	..	..	..	..	..	219

PART II.

WINES 222

Introduction : The Lucky Hour of Great
Wines, by " Colette " 223
The Wines of Bordeaux .. :. 230
Champagne 248
The Wines of Burgundy 258
Hock and Moselle 266
Port 272
Sherry 276

CONCLUDING REMARKS 280

BLANK PAGES FOR ADDITIONS 282

COCKTAILS

HISTORICAL NOTE

MOST of the people one meets in places where Cocktails grow have an idea that they know the origin of the word " Cocktail " ; none of them. however, agree as to what that origin is, and in any case they are all wrong, as they always put that origin somewhere between sixty and seventy years ago, whereas in *The Balance*, an American periodical, of May 13, 1806, we read that : " *Cocktail* is a stimulating liquor, composed of spirits of any kind, sugar, water, and bitters—it is vulgarly called *bittered sling* and is supposed to be an excellent electioneering potion." This is the earliest reference to the Cocktail that I have been able to find in print.

Historians have been misled by the word " Cocktail " into imagining that it was once in some way connected with the plumage of the domestic rooster. But this is not so. The true, authentic and incontrovertible story of the origin of the Cocktail is as follows :—

Somewhere about the beginning of the last century there had been for some time very considerable friction between the American Army of the Southern States and King Axolotl VIII of Mexico. Several skirmishes and one or two

COCKTAILS

battles took place, but eventually a truce was called and the King agreed to meet the American general and to discuss terms of peace with him.

The place chosen for the meeting was the King's Pavilion, and thither the American general repaired, and was accommodated with a seat on the Bench, as it were, next to King A. himself. Before opening negotiations, however, His Majesty asked the general, as one man to another, if he would like a drink, and being an American general he of course said yes. The King gave a command and in a few moments there appeared a lady of entrancing and overwhelming beauty, bearing in her slender fingers a gold cup encrusted with rubies and containing a strange potion of her own brewing. Immediately an awed and ominous hush fell upon the assembly, for the same thought struck everyone at the same time, namely, that as there was only one cup either the King or the general would have to drink out of it first, and that the other would be bound to feel insulted. The situation was growing tense when the cup-bearer seemed also to realize its difficulty, for with a sweet smile she bowed her shapely head in reverence to the assembly and drank the drink herself. Everything was saved and the conference came to a satisfactory ending, but before leaving, the general asked if he might know the name of

COCKTAILS

the lady who had shown such tact. "That," proudly said the King, who had never seen the lady before, "is my daughter Coctel."

"Right," replied the general, "I will see that her name is honoured for evermore by my Army."

Coctel, of course, became Cocktail, and there you are! There exists definite unquestionable proof of the truth of this story, but no correspondence upon the subject can in any circumstances be entertained.

So much for the early history of Cocktails. Since those days the Art of the Cocktail has developed very considerably, and in the following pages you will find the essence of the Art of Harry Craddock of the Savoy, the King of Cocktail Shakers, who has inspired, disciplined, ordered and arranged it. There are few people in the world who can match his vast knowledge of liquids of all kinds, of how to mix them, and of how to create new cocktails for all great or state occasions, so that it is in all confidence that this book is set before you—the confidence that if anything should have been omitted it is in all probability not worth including.

At the same time, a few blank pages have been left at the end of the list of Cocktails for the addition of any new Cocktails that may be invented in the future.

COCKTAILS

THE ABBEY COCKTAIL.

½ Dry Gin. ¼ Kina Lillet.
¼ Orange Juice.
1 Dash Angostura Bitters.
*Shake well and strain into
cocktail glass.*

ABSINTHE COCKTAIL.

½ Absinthe.
½ Water.
1 Dash Syrup.
1 Dash Angostura Bitters.
*Shake well and strain into
cocktail glass*

ABSINTHE (SPECIAL) COCKTAIL.

⅔ Absinthe.
⅙ Gin.
⅙ Syrup of Anisette or
Gomme Syrup.
1 Dash Orange Bitters.
1 Dash Angostura Bitters.
*Shake thoroughly, and strain
into cocktail glass.*

ABSINTHE DRIP COCKTAIL.

1 Liqueur Glass Absinthe.
*Dissolve 1 lump of Sugar, using
the French drip spoon, and fill
glass with cold water.*

COCKTAILS

½ French Vermouth.
½ Italian Vermouth.
*Shake well and strain into
medium size glass and fill with
soda water.   Squeeze orange
peel on top.*

ADDINGTON
COCKTAIL

1 Dash Orange Bitters.
⅓ Italian Vermouth.
⅔ Dry Sherry.
*Stir well and strain into
cocktail glass.*

ADONIS
COCKTAIL.

⅓ French Vermouth.
⅓ Italian Vermouth.
⅓ Scotch Whisky.
2 Dashes Angostura Bitters.
*Stir well and strain into cock-
tail glass.   Squeeze lemon peel
on top.*

AFFINITY
COCKTAIL.

½ Prunelle Brandy.
½ Cherry Brandy.
4 Dashes Lemon Juice.
*Shake well and strain into
sherry glass.*

AFTER
DINNER
COCKTAIL.

½ Apricot Brandy.
½ Curaçao.
*Shake well and strain into
cocktail glass.*

AFTER
DINNER
(SPECIAL)
COCKTAIL.

½ Apricot Brandy.
½ Curaçao.
4 Dashes Lemon Juice.
*Shake well and strain into
cocktail glass.*

AFTER
SUPPER
COCKTAIL.

COCKTAILS

ALASKA COCKTAIL.

¾ Dry Gin.
¼ Yellow Chartreuse.
Shake well and strain into cocktail glass.

So far as can be ascertained this delectable potion is NOT the staple diet of the Esquimaux. It was probably first thought of in South Carolina— hence its name.

ALBERTINE COCKTAIL.
(6 people)

2 Glasses Kirsch.
2 Glasses Cointreau.
2 Glasses Chartreuse.
A Few Drops Maraschino.
Shake well and strain into cocktail glass.

ALEXANDER COCKTAIL. (No. 1.)

½ Dry Gin.
¼ Crème de Cacao.
¼ Sweet Cream.
Shake well and strain into cocktail glass.

ALEXANDER COCKTAIL. (No. 2.)

⅓ Crème de Cacao.
⅓ Brandy. ⅓ Fresh Cream.
Shake well and strain into cocktail glass.

ALEXANDER'S SISTER COCKTAIL.

⅓ Gin. ⅓ Cream.
⅓ Crème de Menthe.
Shake well and strain into cocktail glass.

Ladies are advised to avoid this Cocktail as often as possible.

Put 1 lump of sugar in a medium-sized wine-glass, 2 dashes of Secrestat Bitter poured on to the sugar, 1 lump of ice, ¼ of a glass of Dubonnet, fill remainder with Champagne, squeeze lemon peel on top and stir slightly.	ALFONSO COCKTAIL.
1 Dash Angostura Bitters. 4 Dashes Italian Vermouth. ¼ Dry Gin. ¼ French Vermouth. ½ Grand Marnier. *Shake well and strain into cocktail glass.*	ALFONSO (SPECIAL) COCKTAIL.
½ Italian Vermouth. ½ Russian Kummel. 2 Dashes Scotch Whisky. *Shake well and strain into cocktail glass.*	ALICE MINE COCKTAIL.
1 Dash Lemon Juice. ⅓ Maraschino. ⅔ Plymouth Gin. *Shake well and strain into cocktail glass*	ALLEN (SPECIAL) COCKTAIL.
½ Dry Gin. ½ French Vermouth. 2 Dashes Kummel. *Shake well and strain into cocktail glass.*	ALLIES COCKTAIL.

COCKTAILS

ALMOND COCKTAIL.
(6 people)

Slightly warm 2 Glasses of Gin.
Add a teaspoonful of powdered sugar. Soak in this six peeled almonds and if possible a crushed peach kernel, and allow to cool. When the mixture is cold add a dessertspoonful of Kirsch, one of Peach Brandy, a glass of French Vermouth and 2 glasses of any sweet White Wine.
Shake thoroughly with plenty of ice.

AMERICAN BEAUTY COCKTAIL.

1 Dash Crème de Menthe.
¼ Orange Juice.
¼ Grenadine.
¼ French Vermouth.
¼ Brandy.
Shake well and strain into medium size glass and top with a little port wine.

ANGEL FACE COCKTAIL.

⅓ Dry Gin.
⅓ Apricot Brandy.
⅓ Calvados.
Shake well and strain into cocktail glass.

ANGEL'S KISS COCKTAIL.

¼ Crème de Cacao.
¼ Prunelle Brandy.
¼ Crème de Violette.
¼ Sweet Cream.
Use liqueur Glass and pour carefully, so that ingredients do not mix.

COCKTAILS

¾ Liqueur Glass Crème de
    Cacao.
¼ Fresh Cream.
*Use liqueur glass and float cream
    on top.*

**ANGEL'S
TIP
COCKTAIL.**

½ Crème de Cacao.
½ Prunelle Brandy.
*Use liqueur glass and pour in-
gredients carefully, so that they
do not mix. Pour a little sweet
    cream on top.*

**ANGEL'S
WING
COCKTAIL.**

⅓ Raspberry Syrup.
⅓ Maraschino.
⅓ Crème de Violette.
*Use liqueur glass and pour in-
gredients carefully so that they
    do not mix.*

**ANGEL'S
WINGS
COCKTAIL.**

If the girl does not like it, do not drink it, but
pour it quickly into the nearest flower vase.

2 Dashes Angostura Bitters.
2 Dashes Orange Bitters.
⅓ Hercules. ⅔ Dry Gin.
*Shake well and strain into
    cocktail glass.*

**ANGLER
COCKTAIL.**

1 Dash Angostura Bitters.
¼ Hercules.
¼ Cointreau.
½ Calvados or Apple Brandy.
*Shake well and strain into
    cocktail glass.*

**ANTE
COCKTAIL.**

½ Dry Gin. ½ Dubonnet.
1 Dash Absinthe.
*Shake well and strain into
    cocktail glass.*

**APPARENT
COCKTAIL.**

COCKTAILS

APPETISER COCKTAIL.

½ Gin. ½ Dubonnet.
The Juice of ½ Orange.
Shake well and strain into cocktail glass.

APPLE COCKTAIL. (6 people)

Take 2 glasses of sweet Cider, 1 glass of Gin, 1 glass of Brandy and 2 glasses of Calvados. *Shake and serve.*

This is the Cocktail doctors hate to recommend.

APPLE JACK COCKTAIL.

1 Dash Angostura Bitters.
½ Italian Vermouth.
½ Calvados.
Shake well and strain into cocktail glass.

APPLE JACK (SPECIAL) COCKTAIL.

⅔ Applejack.
⅙ Grenadine.
⅙ Lemon Juice.
Shake well and strain into cocktail glass.

THE APPLE JACK RABBIT COCKTAIL.

1 Hooker of Applejack.
The Juice of 1 Lemon.
The Juice of 1 Orange.
1 Hooker of Maple Syrup
Shake well and strain into cocktail glass.

COCKTAILS

½ Bacardi Rum.
½ Italian Vermouth.
4 Dashes Apricot Brandy.
2 Dashes Grenadine.
4 Dashes Lemon Juice.
*Shake well and strain into
    cocktail glass.*

**APPLE PIE
COCKTAIL.**

¾ Wineglass Rye or Cana-
    dian Club Whisky.
2 Dashes Angostura Bitters.
2 Dashes Curaçao.
*Shake well and strain into wine-
glass. Squeeze lemon and orange
    peel on top.*

**APPROVE
COCKTAIL.**

¼ Lemon Juice.
¼ Orange Juice.
½ Apricot Brandy.
1 Dash Dry Gin.
*Shake well and strain into
    cocktail glass.*

**APRICOT
COCKTAIL**

Cut 2 Apricots in half, break
the stones and let the whole
soak for 2 hours in a glass
and a half of Cognac. Add
two teaspoonfuls of Peach
Bitters, 2 glasses of Gin and
2 glasses of French Ver-
mouth.
*Shake well and strain into
    cocktail glass.*

**APRICOT
COCKTAIL.
(DRY)
(6 people)**

COCKTAILS

APRICOT COCKTAIL.
(SWEET).
(6 people)

Dilute a teaspoonful of apricot jam in a glass of Abricotine. Add a teaspoonful of Peach Bitters, slightly less than two glasses of Gin and 2½ glasses of French Vermouth.
Place this mixture in a shaker and put it on the ice to cool. When quite cold pour in two or three glasses of crushed ice and shake well. Strain into cocktail glass.

ARTILLERY COCKTAIL.

⅓ Italian Vermouth.
⅔ Dry Gin.
Shake well and strain into cocktail glass.

ARTIST'S (SPECIAL) COCKTAIL.

⅓ Whisky. ⅓ Sherry.
⅙ Lemon Juice.
⅙ Groseille Syrup.
Shake well and strain into cocktail glass.

This is the genuine 'Ink of Inspiration' imbibed at the Bal Bullier, Paris. The recipe is from the Artists' Club, Rue Pigalle, Paris.

ASTORIA COCKTAIL.

1 Dash Orange Bitters. ⅔ Gin.
⅓ French Vermouth.
Shake well and strain into cocktail glass.
Serve with stuffed olive.

ATTA BOY COCKTAIL.

⅓ French Vermouth.
⅔ Dry Gin.
4 Dashes Grenadine.
Shake well and strain into cocktail glass.

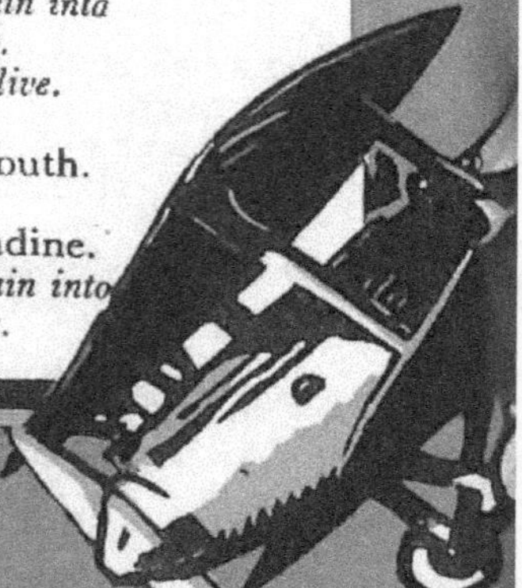

COCKTAILS

¼ French Vermouth.
3 Dashes Absinthe.
¾ Dry Gin.
3 Dashes Crème de Violette.
*Shake well and strain into
cocktail glass.*

**ATTY
COCKTAIL.**

⅓ Lemon Juice. ⅔ Dry Gin.
2 Dashes Maraschino.
*Shake well and strain into
cocktail glass.*

**AVIATION
COCKTAIL.**

1 Dash Gin.
⅓ Sweet Cream.
⅔ Apricot Brandy.
*Shake well and strain into
cocktail glass.*

**BABBIE'S
SPECIAL
COCKTAIL.**

1 Teaspoonful Grenadine.
⅓ Burrough's Beefeater Gin.
⅔ Bacardi Rum.
    The Juice of ½ Lime.
*Shake well and strain into
cocktail glass.*

**BACARDI
SPECIAL
COCKTAIL.***

* Made famous by Karl K. Kitchen, the well-
known New York Newspaper Columnist.

½ Glass Orange Juice.
½ Glass Cointreau.
3 Glasses Sherry.
1 Dash Orange Bitters.
2 Dashes Pimento Dram
    Liqueur.
*Fill up the shaker with cracked
ice, shake and serve with an olive.*

**BALM
COCKTAIL.**
(6 people)

COCKTAILS

BARBARA COCKTAIL.

¼ Fresh Cream.
¼ Crème de Cacao.
½ Vodka.
*Shake well and strain into
cocktail glass.*

THE BARBARY COAST COCKTAIL.

¼ Gin. ¼ Scotch Whisky.
¼ Crème de Cacao.
¼ Cream. Cracked Ice.
Serve in a highball glass.

BARNEY BARNATO COCKTAIL.

1 Dash Angostura Bitters.
1 Dash Curaçao.
½ Caperitif.   ½ Brandy.
*Stir well and strain into
cocktail glass.*

BARON COCKTAIL.

6 Dashes Curaçao.
2 Dashes Italian Vermouth.
⅓ French Vermouth.
⅔ Dry Gin.
*Shake well and strain into
cocktail glass.*

BARTON* SPECIAL COCKTAIL.

¼ Calvados or Apple Brandy.
¼ Scotch Whisky.
½ Dry Gin.
*Shake well and strain into
cocktail glass.*

* What has Bruce Barton got to do with this?

COCKTAILS

Beat up 4 Eggs, and add
4 Glasses of Dry Gin.
⅔ Glass of Cherry Brandy
   or Curaçao.
½ Glass of Lemon Juice.
4 Dashes Orange Bitters.
½ Tablespoonful of Powdered
   Sugar.
1 Tablespoonful of Vanilla
   Flavouring.
*Shake well and strain into
medium-size glass. Grate nutmeg on top. Frost glass with
   castor sugar.*

**BASS
WYATT
COCKTAIL**
(5 people)

⅓ Grenadine. ⅔ Dry Gin.
1 Teaspoonful Fresh Cream.
*Shake well and strain into
   cocktail glass.*

**BELMONT
COCKTAIL.**

2 Dashes Angostura Bitters.
¼ Lime Juice. ¾ Dry Gin.
*Shake well and strain into
   cocktail glass.*

**BENNETT
COCKTAIL.**

½ Calvados, or Apple Brandy.
½ Dubonnet.
*Shake well and strain into
   cocktail glass.*

**BENTLEY
COCKTAIL.**

COCKTAILS

BERRY WALL COCKTAIL.

½ Dry Gin.
½ Italian Vermouth.
4 Dashes Curaçao.
Shake well and strain into cocktail glass. Squeeze lemon peel on top.

BETWEEN-THE-SHEETS COCKTAIL.

1 Dash Lemon Juice.
⅓ Brandy. ⅓ Cointreau.
⅓ Bacardi Rum.
Shake well and strain into cocktail glass.

BICH'S SPECIAL COCKTAIL.

1 Dash Angostura Bitters.
⅓ Kina Lillet. ⅔ Dry Gin.
Shake well and strain into cocktail glass. Squeeze orange peel on top.

BIFFY COCKTAIL.

¼ Lemon Juice.
¼ Swedish Punch. ½ Dry Gin
Shake well and strain into cocktail glass.

BIG BOY COCKTAIL.

½ Brandy. ¼ Cointreau.
¼ Sirop-de-Citron.
Shake well and strain into cocktail glass.

BIJOU COCKTAIL.

⅓ Plymouth Gin.
1 Dash Orange Bitters.
⅓ Green Chartreuse.
⅓ Gancia Italian Vermouth.
Mix well with a spoon in a large bar glass ; strain into a cocktail glass, add a cherry or an olive, squeeze a piece of lemon peel on top and serve.

COCKTAILS

1 Dash Orange Bitters.
¼ Dubonnet.   ¼ Gin.
½ Caperitif.
*Shake well and strain into
   cocktail glass.*

BILTONG
DRY
COCKTAIL.

3 Glasses of Gin.
1½ Glasses of Lemon Juice
      slightly sweetened.
1½ Glasses of Green Chartreuse.
   Before shaking add a
      Dash of Absinthe.
*Shake well and strain into
   cocktail glass.*

BITER
COCKTAIL.
(6 people).

Use long tumbler.
½ Guinness Stout.
½ Champagne.
Pour very carefully.

BLACK
VELVET.

COCKTAILS

BLACKTHORN COCKTAIL.
3 Dashes Angostura Bitters.
3 Dashes Absinthe.
½ Irish Whisky.
½ French Vermouth.
Shake well and strain into cocktail glass.

BLANCHE COCKTAIL.
⅓ Cointreau. ⅓ Anisette.
⅓ White Curaçao.
Shake well and strain into cocktail glass.

BLENTON COCKTAIL.
1 Dash Angostura Bitters.
⅓ French Vermouth.
⅔ Plymouth Gin.
Shake well and strain into cocktail glass.

BLOCK AND FALL COCKTAIL.
⅙ Anis del Oso or Absinthe.
⅙ Calvados. ⅓ Brandy.
⅓ Cointreau.

BLOOD AND SAND COCKTAIL.
¼ Orange Juice.
¼ Scotch Whisky.
¼ Cherry Brandy.
¼ Italian Vermouth.
Shake well and strain into cocktail glass.

BLOOD-HOUND COCKTAIL.
¼ French Vermouth.
¼ Italian Vermouth.
½ Dry Gin.
2 or 3 Crushed Strawberries.
Shake well and strain into cocktail glass.

COCKTAILS

4 Dashes Angostura Bitters. ¾ Wineglassful of Gin. 5 Dashes Orange Curaçao. *Shake well and strain into cocktail glass.*	**BLUE BIRD COCKTAIL.**

BLUE BLAZER.

Use two large silver-plated mugs, with handles.

1 Wineglass Scotch Whisky.

1 Wineglass Boiling Water.

Put the Whisky into one mug, and the boiling water into the other, ignite the Whisky with fire, and while blazing mix both ingredients by pouring them four or five times from one mug to the other. If well done, this will have the appearance of a continued stream of liquid fire.

Sweeten with one teaspoonful of powdered white sugar, and serve in a small bar tumbler, with a piece of lemon peel.

The *Blue Blazer* does not have a very euphonious or classic name, but it tastes better to the palate than it sounds to the ear. A beholder gazing for the first time upon an experienced artist compounding this beverage, would naturally come to the conclusion that it was a nectar for Pluto rather than Bacchus. The novice in mixing this beverage should be careful not to scald himself. To become proficient in throwing the liquid from one mug to the other, it will be necessary to practise for some time with cold water.

½ Dry Gin.
¼ Lemon Juice or Lime
    Juice. ¼ Maraschino.
1 Dash Blue Vegetable
    Extract.
*Shake well and strain into
cocktail glass.*
	**BLUE DEVIL
	COCKTAIL.**

COCKTAILS

BLUE MONDAY COCKTAIL.
¼ Cointreau. ¾ Vodka.
1 Dash Blue Vegetable Extract.
Shake well and strain into cocktail glass.

BLUE TRAIN COCKTAIL.
¼ Lemon Juice.
¼ Cointreau. ½ Dry Gin.
1 Dash of Blue Vegetable Extract.
Shake well and strain into cocktail glass.

THE BLUE TRAIN SPECIAL COCKTAIL.
(6 people)
Fill the shaker with cracked ice and pour into it 1 glass of Brandy and 1 glass of Pineapple syrup. Shake carefully, and then add 3 glasses of Champagne. Give one or two more shakes and serve without further delay.

BLUES COCKTAIL.
(6 people)
Take 4 Glasses of Whisky.
1 Glass of Curaçao.
Incorporate 1 Teaspoonful of Syrup of Prunes.
Pour out over plenty of cracked ice and shake for longer and more thoroughly than usual. Serve very cold.

This Cocktail removes the Blues if you have them and gives you the Blue Devils if you haven't.

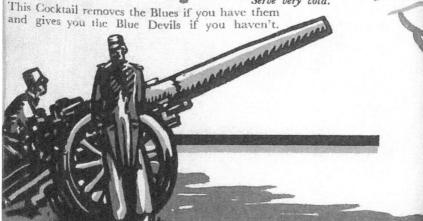

½ Italian Vermouth.
½ Scotch Whisky.
3 Dashes Bénédictine.
Shake well and strain into cocktail glass. Squeeze lemon peel on top.

BOBBY BURNS COCKTAIL.*

*One of the very best Whisky Cocktails. A very fast mover on Saint Andrew's Day.

The Juice of ¼ Lemon or
    ½ Lime.
The Juice of ¼ Orange.
½ Wineglass Bacardi Rum.
1 Teaspoonful Sugar.
Shake well and strain into cocktail glass.

BOLO COCKTAIL.

4 Dashes Lemon Juice.
¾ Wineglass East Indian Punch.
Shake well and strain into cocktail glass.

BOMBAY COCKTAIL. (No. 1.)

1 Dash Absinthe.
2 Dashes Curaçao.
¼ French Vermouth.
¼ Italian Vermouth.
½ Brandy.
Shake well and strain into cocktail glass.

BOMBAY COCKTAIL. (No. 2.)

1 Dash Lemon Juice.
1 Dash Angostura Bitters.
⅓ French Vermouth.
⅓ Canadian Club Whisky.
⅓ Swedish Punch.
Shake well and strain into cocktail glass.

BOOMERANG COCKTAIL.

COCKTAILS

BOOSTER COCKTAIL.

4 Dashes Curaçao.
The White of 1 Egg.
1 Glass Brandy.
Shake well and strain into medium size glass. Nutmeg on top.

BOSOM CARESSER COCKTAIL.*

The Yolk of 1 Egg.
1 Teaspoonful of Grenadine.
⅓ Curaçao. ⅔ Brandy.
Shake well and strain into medium size glass.

*This might be called the " Bobby Jones " or the " Francis Ouimet " Cocktail, as these two gentlemen, usually so chary of expressing preferences, distinctly expressed one for this concoction.

BRAIN-STORM COCKTAIL.

½ Wineglass Irish Whisky.
2 Dashes Bénédictine.
2 Dashes French Vermouth.
Squeeze orange peel on top. Stir well and strain into cocktail glass.

BRANDY COCKTAIL.

2 Dashes Curaçao.
¾ Wineglass Brandy.
Stir well and strain into cocktail glass.

BRANDY BLAZER COCKTAIL.

Use small thick glass.
1 Lump Sugar.
1 Piece of Orange Peel.
1 Piece of Lemon Peel.
1 Glass Brandy.
Light with match, stir with long spoon for a few seconds and strain into cocktail glass.

This can be drunk whilst still alight if so desired.

COCKTAILS

Use small wine glass.
Moisten the edge with lemon
and dip edge into castor sugar
which frosts the glass.
Cut the rind of half a lemon
spiral fashion ; place in glass.
Fill glass with cracked ice.
3 Dashes Maraschino.
1 Dash Angostura Bitters.
4 Dashes Lemon Juice.
$\frac{1}{4}$ Curaçao.
$\frac{3}{4}$ Brandy.
*Stir well and strain into prepared
glass, adding slice of orange.*

**BRANDY
CRUSTA
COCKTAIL.**

1 Hooker of Brandy.
The Juice of 1 Lemon.
2 Dashes Grenadine.
*Shake well and strain into
cocktail glass.*

**BRANDY
GUMP
COCKTAIL.**

3 or 4 Dashes Gomme Syrup.
2 or 3 Dashes Bitters.
1 Wineglass Brandy.
1 or 2 Dashes Curaçao.
*Squeeze lemon peel ; fill one-
third full of ice, and stir with a
spoon.*

**BRANDY
SPECIAL
COCKTAIL.**

1 Dash Angostura Bitters.
$\frac{1}{4}$ Italian Vermouth.
$\frac{3}{4}$ Brandy.
*Stir well and strain into
cocktail glass.*

**BRANDY
VERMOUTH
COCKTAIL.**

COCKTAILS

BRAZIL COCKTAIL.
1 Dash Angostura Bitters.
1 Dash Absinthe.
½ French Vermouth.
½ Sherry.
Stir well and strain into cocktail glass. Squeeze lemon peel on top.

BREAKFAST COCKTAIL.
⅓ Grenadine. ⅔ Dry Gin.
The White of 1 Egg.
Shake well and strain into large wine glass.

BROADWAY SMILE COCKTAIL.
⅓ Crème de Cassis.
⅓ Swedish Punch.
⅓ Cointreau.
Use liqueur glass and pour carefully so that ingredients do not mix.

The Yolk of 1 Egg.
⅛ Gin.
⅛ Gancia Italian Vermouth.
⅔ White Port.
1 Teaspoonful Anisette Marie Brisard.

Shake well and strain into cocktail glass.

BROKEN SPUR
COCKTAIL

The Juice of ¼ Orange.
¼ French Vermouth.
¼ Italian Vermouth.
½ Dry Gin.
Shake well and strain into cocktail glass.

BRONX
COCKTAIL.

The Juice of ¼ Orange.
The White of 1 Egg.
¼ French Vermouth.
¼ Italian Vermouth.
½ Dry Gin.
Shake well and strain into large wine glass.

BRONX
(SILVER)
COCKTAIL.

⅔ Gin. ⅓ French Vermouth.
The Juice of ½ Lime.
Shake well and strain into cocktail glass.

BRONX
TERRACL
COCKTAIL.

37

COCKTAILS

BROOKLYN COCKTAIL.

1 Dash Amer Picon.
1 Dash Maraschino.
⅔ Canadian Club Whisky.
⅓ French Vermouth.
*Shake well and strain into
    cocktail glass.*

BRUNELLE COCKTAIL.

¼ Absinthe.
½ Tablespoonful Sugar.
¾ Lemon Juice.
*Shake well and strain into
    cocktail glass.*

BUDS SPECIAL COCKTAIL.

1 Dash Angostura Bitters.
⅓ Sweet Cream.
⅔ Cointreau.
*Stir well and strain into
    cocktail glass.*

BULL-DOG COCKTAIL.

Put 2 or 3 lumps of Ice into
a large tumbler, add the
juice of 1 Orange, 1 glass of
Gin. Fill balance with
Ginger Ale.
Stir, and serve with a straw.

BUNNY HUG COCKTAIL.

⅓ Gin.   ⅓ Whisky.
⅓ Absinthe.
*Shake well and strain into
    cocktail glass.*

This Cocktail should immediately be poured
down the sink before it is too late.

BUSH-RANGER COCKTAIL.

2 Dashes Angostura Bitters.
½ Caperitif. ½ Bacardi Rum.
*Stir well and strain into
    cocktail glass.*

COCKTAILS

⅓ Bacardi Rum.
⅓ Dry Gin.
⅓ French Vermouth.
*Shake well and strain into
    cocktail glass.*

**B.V.D.
COCKTAIL.**

1 Liqueur Glass Ginger
1 Liqueur Glass Curaçao.
1 Liqueur Glass Port.
1 Liqueur Glass Sherry.
*Shake well and strain into
    cocktail glass.*

**BYCULLA
COCKTAIL.**

⅓ French Vermouth.
⅓ Canadian Club Whisky.
⅓ Byrrh.
*Shake well and strain into
    cocktail glass.*

**BYRRH
COCKTAIL.**

1 Glass Byrrh.
½ Glass Crème de Cassis.
*Use medium size glass and fill up
    with soda water.*

**BYRRH
CASSIS.**

½ Byrrh Wine. ½ Tom Gin.
*Stir well and strain into
    cocktail glass.*

**BYRRH
SPECIAL
COCKTAIL.**

1 Dash Absinthe.
1 Dash Angostura Bitters.
½ Dry Gin. ½ Caperitif.
*Shake well and strain into cock-
    tail glass. Add a cherry.*

**CABARET
COCKTAIL.**

COCKTAILS

CABLEGRAM COCKTAIL.

The Juice of ½ Lemon.
½ Tablespoonful Powdered Sugar.
1 Glass Canadian Club Whisky.
Shake well, strain into long tumbler and fill with Ginger Ale.

CAFÉ DE PARIS COCKTAIL.

The White of 1 Egg.
3 Dashes Anisette.
1 Teaspoonful of Fresh Cream.
1 Glass Dry Gin.
Shake well and strain into medium size glass.

CAFÉ KIRSCH COCKTAIL.

The White of 1 Egg.
1 Liqueur Glass Kirsch.
½ Tablespoonful of Sugar.
1 Small Glass of Cold Coffee.
Shake well and strain into cocktail glass.

**CALVADOS COCKTAIL.
(6 people)**

2 Glasses Calvados.
2 Glasses Orange Juice.
1 Glass Cointreau.
1 Glass Orange Bitters.
Add plenty of ice and shake carefully.

Variation of the above.

3 Glasses Calvados.
3 Glasses Sweetened Lemon Juice.
Shake very thoroughly and serve.

COCKTAILS

⅓ Scotch Whisky.
⅓ Irish Whisky.
⅙ Lemon Juice.
⅙ Orgeat Syrup.
Shake well and strain into cocktail glass.

CAMERON'S KICK COCKTAIL.

½ Dry Gin. ¼ Cointreau.
¼ Kina Lillet.
Shake well and strain into cocktail glass.

CAMPDEN COCKTAIL.

The Juice of ¼ Lemon.
¼ Tablespoonful Powdered Sugar.
1 Liqueur Glass Curaçao.
3 Dashes Jamaica Rum.
Shake well and strain into cocktail glass.

CANADIAN COCKTAIL.

COCKTAILS

CANADIAN WHISKY COCKTAIL.

2 Dashes Angostura Bitters.
2 Teaspoonsful Gomme Syrup.
1 Glass Canadian Club Whisky.
Shake well and strain into cocktail glass.

CAPE COCKTAIL.

⅓ Dry Gin. ⅓ Caperitif.
⅓ Orange Juice.
Shake well and strain into cocktail glass.

CAPETOWN COCKTAIL.

1 Dash Angostura Bitters.
3 Dashes Curaçao.
½ Caperitif.
½ Canadian Club Whisky.
Stir well and strain into cocktail glass. Lemon peel on top.

CARROL COCKTAIL.

⅔ Brandy.
⅓ Italian Vermouth.
Stir well and strain into cocktail glass. Add pickled walnut or onion.

CARUSO COCKTAIL.

⅓ Dry Gin.
⅓ French Vermouth.
⅓ Green Crème de Menthe.
Shake well and strain into cocktail glass.

CASINO COCKTAIL.

2 Dashes Maraschino.
2 Dashes Orange Bitters.
2 Dashes Lemon Juice.
1 Glass Old Tom Gin.
Stir well and add cherry.

CASTLE DIP COCKTAIL.

½ Apple Brandy.
½ White Crème de Menthe.
3 Dashes Absinthe.
Shake well and strain into cocktail glass.

CATS-EYE COCKTAIL.
(6 people)

½ Glass Fresh Lemonade.
½ Glass Water.
2 Glasses Gin.
1 Dessertspoonful Kirsch.
½ Glass Cointreau.
Not quite 2 Glasses French Vermouth.
Shake well and strain into cocktail glasses. Serve with an olive.

CECIL PICK-ME-UP COCKTAIL.

The Yolk of 1 Egg.
1 Glass Brandy.
1 Teaspoonful Castor Sugar.
Shake well and strain into medium-size wine glass and fill balance with Ayala Champagne.

C.F.H. COCKTAIL.

⅙ Grenadine.
⅙ Cederlund's Swedish Punch.
⅙ Calvados. ⅙ Lemon Juice.
⅓ Burrough's Beefeater Gin.

CHAMPAGNE COCKTAIL.

Put into a wine glass one lump of Sugar, and saturate it with Angostura Bitters. Having added to this 1 lump of Ice, fill the glass with Champagne, squeeze on top a piece of lemon peel, and serve with a slice of orange.

COCKTAILS

CHAMPS ELYSÉES COCKTAIL.
(6 people)

3 Glasses Cognac.
1 Glass Chartreuse.
1½ Glasses Sweetened Lemon Juice.
1 Dash Angostura Bitters.
Shake well and strain into cocktail glasses.

CHANTI-CLER COCKTAIL.

The Juice of ½ Lemon.
1 Tablespoonful Raspberry Syrup.
The White of 1 Egg.
1 Glass Dry Gin.
Shake well and strain into medium size glass.

CHARLES COCKTAIL.

1 Dash Angostura Bitters.
½ Italian Vermouth.
½ Brandy.
Stir well and strain into cocktail glass.

This is the only known authentic Jacobite Cocktail.

CHARLESTON COCKTAIL.

⅙ Dry Gin.   ⅙ Glass Kirsch.
⅙ Glass Maraschino.
⅙ Glass Curaçao.
⅙ French Vermouth.
⅙ Italian Vermouth.
Shake well and strain into cocktail glass. Squeeze Lemon Peel on top.

COCKTAILS

To a glass half full of cracked ice add a tablespoonful of dry Curaçao, one of Lemon Juice, one of Grenadine, 2½ glasses of Cherry Brandy and 2 of Brandy. *Shake thoroughly and serve very cold.*

CHERRY BLOSSOM COCKTAIL.
(6 people)

1 Dash Angostura Bitters.
1 Dash Maraschino.
½ French Vermouth.
½ Italian Vermouth.
Shake well and strain into cocktail glass.
Serve with cherry.

CHERRY MIXTURE COCKTAIL.

1 Dash Angostura Bitters.
1 Dash Curaçao.
⅔ Brandy.
Shake well and strain into cocktail glass. Frost edge of glass with castor sugar and fill with Champagne.

CHICAGO COCKTAIL.

1 Dash Angostura Bitters.
3 Dashes Maraschino.
3 Dashes Curaçao.
⅓ Grenadine.
⅔ Jamaica Rum.
Shake well and strain into cocktail glass.

CHINESE COCKTAIL.

COCKTAILS

CHOCOLATE COCKTAIL. (No. 1.)

1 Teaspoonful Powdered Chocolate.
1 Egg.
1 Liqueur Glass Maraschino.
1 Liqueur Glass Yellow Chartreuse.
Shake well and strain into large glass.

CHOCOLATE COCKTAIL. (No. 2.)

The Yolk of 1 Fresh Egg.
$\frac{1}{4}$ Yellow Chartreuse.
$\frac{3}{4}$ Port Wine.
Teaspoonful of Crushed Chocolate.
Shake well and strain into medium size glass.

CHOKER COCKTAIL.* (6 people)

4 Glasses Whisky.
2 Glasses Absinthe.
1 Dash Absinthe Bitters.
This Cocktail is to be very thoroughly shaken and no sweetening in any form should be added.

*Drink this and you can drink anything : new-laid eggs put into it immediately become hard-boiled.

CHORUS LADY COCKTAIL

The Juice of $\frac{1}{4}$ Orange.
$\frac{1}{3}$ Dry Gin.
$\frac{1}{3}$ Italian Vermouth.
$\frac{1}{3}$ French Vermouth.
Shake well and strain into medium-size glass. Add slice of orange and a cherry.

COCKTAILS

3 Dashes Absinthe.
⅓ Bénédictine.
⅔ French Vermouth.
*Shake well and strain into cocktail
glass. Squeeze orange peel on top.*

**CHRYSAN-
THEMUM
COCKTAIL.***

*Well-known and very popular in the American
Bar of the S.S. " Europa."

⅔ Plymouth Gin.
1 Dash Orange Curaçao.
4 Dashes Orange Juice.
⅓ French Vermouth.
*Shake well and strain into
cocktail glass.*

**CHURCH
PARADE
COCKTAIL.**

2 Dashes Angostura.
2 Dashes Orange Bitters.
1 Glass Cinzano Vermouth.
*Shake well and strain into cock-
tail glass, and squeeze orange
peel on top.*

**CINZANO
COCKTAIL.**

In a wineglass put 1 lump of
Sugar, 2 dashes of Angostura,
1 dash of Curaçao, 1 tea-
spoonful Brandy, 1 lump of
Ice.
*Fill up with Cinzano Brut, stir
slightly, and squeeze lemon peel
on top.*

**CINZANO
SPARKLING
COCKTAIL.**

⅓ Dry Gin.
⅓ French Vermouth.
⅙ Apricot Brandy.
⅙ Cointreau.
*Shake well and strain into
cocktail glass.*

**CLARIDGE
COCKTAIL.**

COCKTAILS

CLASSIC COCKTAIL.

⅙ Lemon Juice.
⅙ Curaçao.
⅙ Maraschino.
½ Brandy.
Shake well and strain into cocktail glass.
Frost rim of glass with castor sugar. Squeeze lemon peel on top.

CLAYTON'S SPECIAL COCKTAIL.

½ Bacardi Rum. .
¼ Kola Tonic.
¼ Sirop-de-Citron.
Shake well and strain into cocktail glass.

CLOVER CLUB COCKTAIL.

The Juice of ½ Lemon.
  or of 1 Lime.
⅓ Grenadine.
  The White of 1 Egg.
⅔ Dry Gin.
Shake well and strain into medium size glass.

CLOVER LEAF COCKTAIL.

The same as *CLOVER CLUB*, with a sprig of fresh Mint on top.

CLUB COCKTAIL.

⅔ Dry Gin.
⅓ Italian Vermouth.
1 Dash Yellow Chartreuse.
Shake well and strain into cocktail glass.

Portrait of Sir Frederick Popplehaugh, Bart., of Yorkshire, President of the Clover Club.

The Yolk of 1 Egg.
1 Teaspoonful Sugar or Gomme Syrup.
⅓ Port Wine.
⅛ Brandy.
1 Dash Curaçao.
Shake well, strain into a small wineglass, and grate a little nutmeg on top.

COFFEE COCKTAIL.*

* The name of this drink is a misnomer, as coffee is not to be found among its ingredients, but it looks like coffee when it has been properly concocted.

¼ White Crème de Menthe.
¼ Italian Vermouth.
½ Brandy.
Shake well and strain into cocktail glass.

COLD DECK COCKTAIL.

⅔ Dry Gin.
⅓ Grape Fruit Juice.
3 Dashes Maraschino.
Shake well and strain into cocktail glass.

COLONIAL COCKTAIL.

COCKTAILS

COMMODORE COCKTAIL.

1 Teaspoonful Syrup.
2 Dashes Orange Bitters.
The Juice of ½ Lime or ¼ Lemon.
1 Glass Canadian Club Whisky.
Shake well and strain into cocktail glass.

COOPERS-TOWN COCKTAIL.

⅓ French Vermouth.
⅓ Italian Vermouth.
⅓ Dry Gin.
Shake well and strain into cocktail glass. Add a sprig of Mint.

CORDOVA COCKTAIL.

⅔ Dry Gin.
1 Dash Absinthe.
1 Teaspoonful Fresh Cream.
⅓ Italian Vermouth.
Shake well and strain into cocktail glass.

THE CORN POPPER

1 Pint Corn (Georgia or Maryland).
½ Pint Cream.
The Whites of 2 Eggs.
1 Tablespoonful Grenadine.
Fill highball glasses half full of this mixture and fill up with Vichy or Seltzer.

THE CORNELL SPECIAL COCKTAIL.

¼ Part Gin.
¼ Part Bénédictine.
¼ Part Lemon.
¼ Part Lithia Water.
Stir well and serve in cocktail glass.

COCKTAILS

½ Sherry.
½ French Vermouth.
1 Dash Maraschino.
2 Dashes Orange Bitters.
Shake well and strain into cocktail glass.

CORONATION COCKTAIL. (No. 1.)

1 Dash Peppermint.
1 Dash Peach Bitters.
3 Dashes Curaçao.
⅔ Brandy.
Shake well and strain into cocktail glass.

CORONATION COCKTAIL. (No. 2.)

¼ Italian Vermouth.
¼ Apple Brandy or Calvados.
½ Brandy.
Shake well and strain into cocktail glass.

CORPSE REVIVER. (No. 1.)

To be taken before 11 a.m., or whenever steam and energy are needed.

COCKTAILS

CORPSE REVIVER (No. 2.)	¼ Wine Glass Lemon Juice. ¼ Wine Glass Kina Lillet. ¼ Wine Glass Cointreau. ¼ Wine Glass Dry Gin. 1 Dash Absinthe. *Shake well and strain into cocktail glass.*

Four of these taken in swift succession will unrevive the corpse again.

COTA COCKTAIL.	¼ Hercules. ¼ Cointreau. ½ Dry Gin. *Shake well and strain into cocktail glass.*
COUNTRY CLUB COOLER.	1 Glass French Vermouth. 1 Teaspoonful Grenadine. 2 Lumps of Ice. *Pour into tumbler and fill up with soda water.*
THE COWBOY COCKTAIL.	⅔ Whisky. ⅓ Cream. Cracked Ice. *Shake well and strain into cocktail glass.*
CREOLE COCKTAIL.	½ Rye or Canadian Club Whisky. ½ Italian Vermouth. 2 Dashes Bénédictine. 2 Dashes Amer Picon. *Stir well and strain into cocktail glass. Twist lemon peel on top.*

COCKTAILS

⅓ Whisky.
⅔ Lemon Juice.
1 Dash Grenadine.
*Shake well and strain into
cocktail glass.*

**THE CROW
COCKTAIL.**

The Juice of ¼ Orange.
¼ French Vermouth.
¼ Italian Vermouth.
1 Lump Ice.
*Use medium-size glass and fill
up with Soda Water.*

**CRYSTAL
BRONX
COCKTAIL.**

The Juice of ¼ Lemon.
1 Teaspoonful Powdered
Sugar.
1 Glass Bacardi Rum.
*Shake well and strain into
cocktail glass.*

**CUBAN
COCKTAIL.
(No. 1.)**

The Juice of ½ Lime or ¼
Lemon.
⅓ Apricot Brandy.
⅔ Brandy.
*Shake well and strain into
cocktail glass.*

**CUBAN
COCKTAIL.
(No. 2.)**

½ Gin. ½ Vermouth.
4 Drops Kummel.
4 Drops Charbreux.
2 Drops Pineapple Syrup.
*Shake well and strain into
cocktail glass.*

**THE CUBANO
COCKTAIL.**

COCKTAILS

THE CULROSS COCKTAIL.

The Juice of ¼ Lemon.
⅓ Kina Lillet.
⅓ Bacardi Rum.
⅓ Apricot Brandy.
Shake well and strain into cocktail glass.

CUPID COCKTAIL.

1 Glass Sherry.
1 Fresh Egg.
Teaspoonful Powdered Sugar.
A little Cayenne Pepper.
Shake well and strain into medium size glass

CURACAO COCKTAIL. (6 people)

½ Glass Brandy.
2½ Glasses Dark Curaçao.
2½ Glasses Orange Juice.
½ Glass Gin.
Broken Ice.
Shake and serve in glasses rinsed out with Orange Bitters.

DAIQUIRI COCKTAIL.

The Juice of ¼ Lemon or ½ Lime.
1 Teaspoonful Powdered Sugar.
1 Glass Bacardi Rum.
Shake well and strain into cocktail glass.

" The moment had arrived for a *Daiquiri*. It was a delicate compound ; it elevated my contentment to an even higher pitch. Unquestionably the cocktail on my table was a dangerous agent, for it held in its shallow glass bowl slightly encrusted

COCKTAILS

with undissolved sugar the power of a contemptuous indifference to fate ; it set the mind free of responsibility ; obliterating both memory and tomorrow, it gave the heart an adventitious feeling of superiority and momentarily vanquished all the celebrated, the eternal fears. Yes, that was the danger of skilfully prepared intoxicating drinks . . . The word 'intoxicating' adequately expressed their power, their menace to orderly, monotonous resignation. A word, I thought further, debased by moralists from its primary ecstatic content . . . but then, with a fresh *Daiquiri* and a sprig of orange blossom in my button-hole, it meant less than nothing."

A short extract from Joseph Hergesheimer's "San Cristobal de la Habana," which contains much wisdom concerning Drinks, Cigars and the Art of Fine Living.

(Quoted by kind permission of the publishers, Messrs. William Heineman Ltd., and Messrs. Alfred A. Knopf, Inc.)

3 Dashes Curaçao.
¼ Orange Juice.
¼ Italian Vermouth.
½ Dry Gin.
Shake well and strain into cocktail glass.

DAMN-THE-
WEATHER
COCKTAIL.

COCKTAILS

DANDY COCKTAIL.

½ Rye or Canadian Club Whisky.
½ Dubonnet.
1 Dash Angostura Bitters.
3 Dashes Cointreau.
1 Piece Lemon Peel.
1 Piece Orange Peel.
Shake well and strain into cocktail glass.

DARB COCKTAIL.

⅓ French Vermouth.
⅓ Dry Gin.
⅓ Apricot Brandy.
4 Dashes Lemon Juice.
Shake well and strain into cocktail glass.

DAVIS COCKTAIL.

¼ Jamaica Rum.
½ French Vermouth.
2 Dashes Grenadine.
Juice of ½ Lemon or 1 Lime.
Shake well and strain into cocktail glass.

DAVIS BRANDY COCKTAIL.

1 Dash Angostura Bitters.
4 Dashes Grenadine.
⅓ French Vermouth.
⅔ Brandy.
Shake well and strain into cocktail glass.

DEAUVILLE COCKTAIL.

¼ Brandy.
¼ Calvados.
¼ Cointreau.
¼ Lemon Juice.
Shake well and strain into cocktail glass.

COCKTAILS

1 Dash Absinthe.
1 Dash Orange Bitters.
½ French Vermouth.
½ Old Tom Gin.
Shake well and strain into cocktail glass. Add 1 olive and squeeze Lemon Peel on top.

DEEP SEA COCKTAIL.

2 Dashes Absinthe
2 Dashes Grenadine.
½ Gin. ½ Calvados.
Shake well and strain into cocktail glass.

DEMPSEY COCKTAIL.

2 Dashes Absinthe.
½ Glass Kina Lillet.
½ Glass Dry Gin.
Shake well and strain into cocktail glass.
Squeeze orange peel on top.

DEPTH CHARGE COCKTAIL.

Carefully shake together 2½ glasses of Brandy, and the same amount of Calvados to which has been added 2 dessertspoonsful of Grenadine and 4 of Lemon Juice.

DEPTH-CHARGE BRANDY COCKTAIL.
(6 people)

1 Dash Lemon Juice.
4 Dashes Grenadine.
½ Calvados or Apple Brandy.
½ Brandy.
Shake well and strain into cocktail glass.

DEPTH BOMB COCKTAIL.

Two favourite War-time Cocktails. They owed their inspiration to the activities of the famous M.L. Submarine Chasers during the hostilities.

COCKTAILS

DERBY COCKTAIL.
2 Dashes Peach Bitters.
2 Sprigs Fresh Mint.
1 Glass Dry Gin.
Shake well and strain into cocktail glass.

DE RIGUEUR COCKTAIL.
½ Whisky.
¼ Grape Fruit Juice.
¼ Honey.
Cracked Ice.
Shake well and strain into cocktail glass.

DESERT HEALER COCKTAIL.
The Juice of 1 Orange.
1 Glass Dry Gin.
½ Liqueur Glass Cherry Brandy.
Shake well and strain into long tumbler and fill with Ginger Beer.

DEVIL'S COCKTAIL.
½ Port Wine.
½ French Vermouth.
2 Dashes Lemon Juice.
Shake well and strain into cocktail glass.

COCKTAILS

Pour into the shaker 4 glasses of Sparkling Cider and 2 glasses of Gin. Add some ice and a few drops of Orange Bitters.
Shake lightly and serve.

DEVONIA COCKTAIL.
(6 people)

$\frac{2}{3}$ Dubonnet.
$\frac{1}{3}$ Gin.
2 Dashes Orgeat Syrup.
Shake well and strain into cocktail glass.

DIABOLA COCKTAIL.

Pour into the shaker 3 glasses of Brandy and 3 of French Vermouth. Add a spoonful of Angostura and 2 spoonsful of Orange Bitters.
Shake and serve with piece of lemon rind and an olive, or, if preferred, a cherry.

DIABOLO COCKTAIL.
(6 people)

Use Port Wine Glass.
Fill with Shaved Ice.
Fill Glass $\frac{3}{4}$ full with White Crème de Menthe and top with Brandy.

DIANA COCKTAIL.

$\frac{1}{6}$ Grape Fruit Juice.
$\frac{1}{6}$ Swedish Punch.
$\frac{2}{3}$ Calvados.
Shake well and strain into cocktail glass.

DIKI-DIKI COCKTAIL.

DINAH COCKTAIL. (6 people)

First put 2 or 3 sprigs of fresh mint in the shaker and bruise them lightly against the sides of the shaker by stirring with a silver spoon. Pour into the shaker 3 glasses of Whisky and let it stand for some minutes. Add 3 glasses of sweetened Lemon Juice and some ice. Shake very carefully and for longer than usual. Serve with a mint leaf standing in each glass.

DIPLOMAT COCKTAIL.

1 Dash Maraschino.
2/3 French Vermouth.
1/3 Italian Vermouth.
Shake well and strain into cocktail glass. Add cherry and squeeze lemon peel on top.

DIXIE COCKTAIL.

1/2 Dry Gin.
1/4 French Vermouth.
1/4 Absinthe.
Shake well and strain into cocktail glass.

COCKTAILS

DIXIE WHISKY COCKTAIL.
(6 people)

To 2 lumps of sugar add a small teaspoon of Angostura Bitters, another of Lemon Juice, 4 glasses of Whisky, a small teaspoonful of Curaçao and 2 teaspoonsful of Crème de Menthe. Add plenty of ice and shake carefully. *Serve.*

DOCTOR COCKTAIL.

⅓ Lemon Juice or Lime Juice.
⅔ Swedish Punch.
Shake well and strain into cocktail glass.

THE DODGE SPECIAL COCKTAIL.

½ Gin.
½ Cointreau or Mint.
1 Dash Grape Juice.
Shake well and strain into cocktail glass.

COCKTAILS

DOLLY O'DARE COCKTAIL.

6 Dashes Apricot Brandy.
½ French Vermouth.
½ Dry Gin.
Shake well and strain into cocktail glass. Squeeze orange peel on top.

DOUGLAS COCKTAIL.

⅓ French Vermouth.
⅔ Plymouth Gin.
Shake well and strain into cocktail glass. Squeeze orange and lemon peel on top.

DREAM COCKTAIL.

⅓ Curaçao.
⅔ Brandy.
1 Dash Absinthe.
Shake well and strain into cocktail glass.

DRY MARTINI COCKTAIL.

½ French Vermouth.
½ Gin.
1 Dash Orange Bitters.
Shake well and strain into cocktail glass.

DU BARRY COCKTAIL.

1 Dash Angostura Bitters.
2 Dashes Absinthe.
⅓ French Vermouth.
⅔ Plymouth Gin.
Shake well and strain into cocktail glass. Add slice of orange.

DUBONNET COCKTAIL.

½ Dubonnet.
½ Dry Gin.
Stir well and strain into cocktail glass.

COCKTAILS

⅓ French Vermouth.
⅓ Italian Vermouth.
⅓ Absinthe.
*Shake well and strain into
  cocktail glass.*

**DUCHESS
COCKTAIL.**

½ Sherry.
½ Italian Vermouth.
3 Dashes Orange Bitters.
*Stir well and twist orange peel
  on top.*

**DUKE OF
MARL-
BOROUGH
COCKTAIL.**

In a shaker filled with
cracked Ice place a spoonful
of Curaçao, 2 glasses of Gin,
2 glasses of Sherry, 2 glasses
of French Vermouth.
*Stir thoroughly with a spoon,
shake, strain, and serve. Add
an olive and 2 dashes of
Absinthe to each glass.*

**DUNHILL'S
SPECIAL
COCKTAIL**
(6 people)

1 Dash Angostura Bitters.
⅓ Sherry. ⅔ Rum.
*Stir well and strain into
  cocktail glass.*

**DUNLOP
COCKTAIL.**

Pour 4½ glasses of Whisky
into a large glass and soak in
this a few cloves. Add 5 or
6 drops of Orange Bitters,
and lastly put in 1½ glasses of
Curaçao.
*Place the lot in the shaker;
shake and serve.*

**DUPPY
COCKTAIL.**
(6 people)

| EAGLE'S DREAM COCKTAIL. | 1 Teaspoonful of Powdered Sugar.
The White of 1 Egg.
The Juice of ¼ Lemon.
¼ Crème Yvette.
¾ Dry Gin.
Shake well and strain into medium size glass. |

| THE EARTH-QUAKE* COCKTAIL. | ⅓ Gin.   ⅓ Whisky.
⅓ Absinthe.
Shake well and serve in cocktail glass. |

* So-called because if there *should* happen to be an earthquake on when you are drinking it, it won't matter.

This is a Cocktail whose potency is not to be taken too lightly, or, for that matter, too frequently!

| EAST AND WEST COCKTAIL. | 1 Dash Lemon Juice.
¼ Bacardi Rum.
¾ East India Punch.
Shake well and strain into cocktail glass. |

Created to mark the arrival in London of a Ruling Indian Prince.

| EAST INDIA COCKTAIL. | ⅛ Pineapple Juice.
⅛ Orange Curaçao.
1 Dash Angostura Bitters.
¾ Brandy.
Stir well and strain into cocktail glass. |

COCKTAILS

Equal parts of French Vermouth and Sherry, with a dash of Orange Bitters.
Shake well and strain into cocktail glass.

EAST INDIAN COCKTAIL.

⅓ Dry Gin.   ⅔ Sloe Gin.
Put enough Grenadine in a cocktail glass to cover a ripe olive. Mix the spirits together and pour gently on to the Grenadine so that it does not mix. Squeeze orange peel on top.

ECLIPSE COCKTAIL.

2 Dashes Apricot Brandy.
⅓ Glass Kina Lillet.
⅔ Glass Dry Gin.
Shake well and strain into cocktail glass. Squeeze lemon peel on top.

EDDIE BROWN COCKTAIL.

COCKTAILS

ELK COCKTAIL.

½ Prunelle Brandy.
2 Dashes French Vermouth.
½ Dry Gin.
Shake well and strain into cocktail glass.

ELK'S OWN COCKTAIL.

The White of 1 Egg.
½ Canadian Club Whisky.
½ Port Wine.
The Juice of ½ Lemon.
1 Teaspoonful Sugar.
Shake well, strain into wineglass and add a slice of pineapple.

ELIXIR COCKTAIL.

½ Kola Tonic.
½ Calvados.
Shake well and strain into cocktail glass.

EMPIRE COCKTAIL.

¼ Apricot Brandy.
¼ Calvados. ½ Gin.
Shake well and strain into cocktail glass.

E. NOS COCKTAIL.

⅓ French Vermouth.
⅔ Nicholson's Gin.
3 Dashes of Absinthe.
Shake well and strain into cocktail glass.

ETHEL COCKTAIL.

⅓ Apricot Brandy.
⅓ White Crème de Menthe.
⅓ Curaçao.
Shake well and strain into cocktail glass.

COCKTAILS

The Juice of ½ Lemon.
½ Tablespoonful of Powdered
Sugar. ¼ Kirsch.
¾ Plymouth Gin.
*Shake well and strain into long
tumbler ; fill up with soda-
water.*

ETON
BLAZER
COCKTAIL.

3 Dashes Green Mint.
6 Dashes Green Chartreuse.
Irish Whisky.
Add a Green Olive.

" EVERY-
BODY'S
IRISH "
COCKTAIL.

Created to mark, and now in great demand on,
St. Patrick's Day. The green olive suspended in
the liquid, looks like a gibbous moon.

¼ Whisky. ¼ Gin.
¼ Lemon Juice.
¼ Orange Juice.
1 Egg.
1 Teaspoonful of Apricot
Brandy.
Powdered Sugar.
*Shake well and strain into
cocktail glass.*

" EVERY-
THING
BUT "
COCKTAIL.

The Yolk of 1 Fresh Egg.
1 Teaspoonful Powdered
Sugar.
2 Dashes Absinthe.
2 Dashes Curaçao.
2 Dashes Crème de Noyau.
1 Liqueur Glass Rum.
*Shake well and strain into
cocktail glass.*

EYE-
OPENER
COCKTAIL.

COCKTAILS

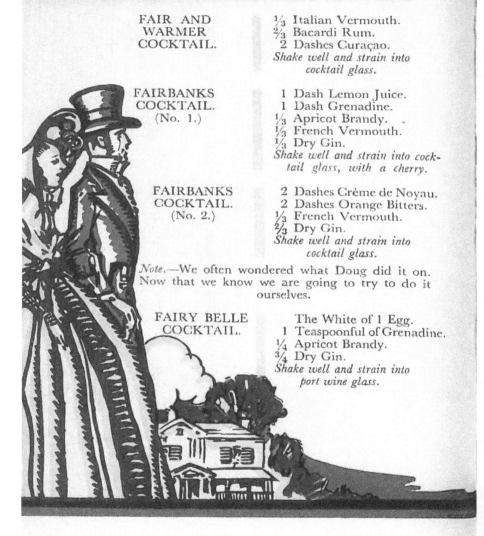

FAIR AND
WARMER
COCKTAIL.

1/3 Italian Vermouth.
2/3 Bacardi Rum.
2 Dashes Curaçao.
Shake well and strain into cocktail glass.

FAIRBANKS
COCKTAIL.
(No. 1.)

1 Dash Lemon Juice.
1 Dash Grenadine.
1/3 Apricot Brandy.
1/3 French Vermouth.
1/3 Dry Gin.
Shake well and strain into cocktail glass, with a cherry.

FAIRBANKS
COCKTAIL.
(No. 2.)

2 Dashes Crème de Noyau.
2 Dashes Orange Bitters.
1/3 French Vermouth.
2/3 Dry Gin.
Shake well and strain into cocktail glass.

Note.—We often wondered what Doug did it on. Now that we know we are going to try to do it ourselves.

FAIRY BELLE
COCKTAIL.

The White of 1 Egg.
1 Teaspoonful of Grenadine.
1/4 Apricot Brandy.
3/4 Dry Gin.
Shake well and strain into port wine glass.

COCKTAILS

FALLEN ANGEL COCKTAIL.

1 Dash Angostura Bitters.
2 Dashes Crème de Menthe.
The Juice of 1 Lemon or ½ Lime.
1 Glass Dry Gin.
Shake well and strain into cocktail glass.

It has never been made quite clear as to whether this is intended to be taken by the Angel before or after falling; as an encouragement or as a consolation.

FANCY COCKTAIL. (6 people)

Pour into the shaker 5 glasses of Cognac and a dessert-spoonful of Angostura Bitters. Shake thoroughly and serve, adding a little Champagne and a piece of lemon-rind after having rubbed the edges of the glasses with lemon syrup.

FANTASIO COCKTAIL. (No. 1.)

⅙ White Crème de Menthe.
⅙ Maraschino. ⅓ Brandy.
⅓ Dry Gin.
Stir well and strain into cocktail glass.

FANTASIO COCKTAIL. (No. 2.)

⅙ White Crème de Menthe.
⅙ Maraschino.
⅓ Brandy. ⅓ Dry Gin.
Shake well and strain into cocktail glass.

COCKTAILS

FASCINATOR COCKTAIL.

2 Dashes Absinthe.
⅓ French Vermouth.
⅔ Dry Gin.
1 Sprig Fresh Mint.
Shake well and strain into cocktail glass.

FAVOURITE COCKTAIL.

1 Dash Lemon Juice.
⅓ Apricot Brandy.
⅓ French Vermouth.
⅓ Dry Gin.
Shake well and strain into cocktail glass.

FERNET BRANCA COCKTAIL.

¼ Fernet Branca.
¼ Italian Vermouth.
½ Dry Gin.
Shake well and strain into cocktail glass.

One of the best " morning-after " cocktails ever invented. Fernet-Branca, an Italian vegetable extract, is a marvellous headache cure. (*No advt.*)

FIFTH AVENUE COCKTAIL.

⅓ Crème de Cacao.
⅓ Apricot Brandy.
⅓ Sweet Cream.
Use liqueur glass and pour carefully, so that ingredients do not mix.

FIFTY-FIFTY COCKTAIL.

½ Dry Gin.
½ French Vermouth.
Shake well and strain into cocktail glass.

COCKTAILS

½ Brandy. ¼ Kola Tonic.
¼ Sirop-de-Citron.
*Shake and strain into
cocktail glass.*

**FILMOGRAPH
COCKTAIL.**

¼ Lemon Juice.
¼ Cointreau.
½ Plymouth Gin.
1 Dash Angostura Bitters.
*Shake well and strain into
cocktail glass.*

**FINE
AND DANDY
COCKTAIL.**

⅓ Curaçao.
⅓ French Vermouth.
⅓ Sweet Cream.
*Shake well and strain into
cocktail glass.*

**FIVE-FIFTEEN
COCKTAIL.**

Juice of ¼ Lemon.
1 Dash Jamaica Ginger.
1 Teaspoonful Rock Candy Syrup.
1 Teaspoonful Ginger Brandy.
1 Glass Canadian Club Whisky.
Stir well and strain into cocktail glass, but do not ice.

**'FLU
COCKTAIL.**

Cocktails à la mode. A Cocktail Party in the Very Best Manner of the Period.

COCKTAILS

FLUFFY RUFFLES COCKTAIL.

½ Bacardi Rum.
½ Italian Vermouth.
  The Peel of 1 Lime or Piece of Lemon.
Shake well and strain into cocktail glass.

FLYING SCOTCHMAN COCKTAIL. (6 people)

2½ Glasses Italian Vermouth.
3 Glasses Scotch Whisky.
1 Tablespoonful Bitters.
1 Tablespoonful Sugar Syrup.
Shake well and strain into cocktail glass.

FOUR FLUSH COCKTAIL.

1 Dash Grenadine or Syrup.
¼ French Vermouth.
¼ Swedish Punch.
½ Bacardi Rum.
Shake well and strain into cocktail glass.

FOURTH DEGREE COCKTAIL.

⅓ French Vermouth.
⅓ Gin.
⅓ Italian Vermouth.
4 Dashes of Absinthe.
Shake well and strain into cocktail glass.

FOX RIVER COCKTAIL.

4 Dashes Peach Bitters.
1 Lump of Ice.
¼ Crème de Cacao.
¾ Canadian Club Whisky.
Use wineglass, and squeeze lemon peel on top.

COCKTAILS

The Juice of ½ Lemon or
   1 Lime.
2 Dashes Orange Curaçao.
Bacardi Rum.
Shake well and strain into
   cocktail glass.

**FOX TROT
COCKTAIL.**

⅓ Gin. ⅓ French Vermouth.
⅙ Apricot Brandy.
⅙ Cointreau.
Shake well and strain into
   cocktail glass.

**THE
FRANKEN-
JACK
COCKTAIL.**

¼ Glass Lemon Juice.
¼ Glass Kina Lillet.
¼ Glass Cointreau.
¼ Glass Brandy.
Shake well and strain into
   cocktail glass.

**FRANK
SULLIVAN
COCKTAIL.**

⅔ Gin. ⅓ Lemon Juice.
1 Spoonful Powdered Sugar.
Pour into tall glass containing
cracked Ice and fill up with
   Champagne.
   Hits with remarkable precision.

**THE
FRENCH " 75 "
COCKTAIL.**

The White of 1 Egg.
1 Teaspoonful Grenadine.
1 Glass Plymouth Gin.
Shake well and strain into port
   wine glass.

**FROTH
BLOWER
COCKTAIL.**

1 Teaspoonful Bénédictine.
½ Italian Vermouth.
½ Brandy.
Stir well and strain into cocktail glass.

**FROUPE
COCKTAIL.**

COCKTAILS

FULL HOUSE COCKTAIL.

¼ Swedish Punch.
¼ French Vermouth.
½ Bacardi Rum.
Shake well and strain into cocktail glass.

GANGADINE COCKTAIL.

1 Teaspoonful Framboise Syrup.
⅓ Oxygenée Cusenier.
⅓ White Mint. ⅓ Gin.
Shake well and strain into cocktail glass.

GASPER COCKTAIL. (6 people)

3 Glasses Gin.
3 Glasses Absinthe.
  Add, if required, a very little sugar.
Shake well and serve.

GAZETTE COCKTAIL.

1 Teaspoonful Syrup.
1 Teaspoonful Lemon Juice.
½ Italian Vermouth.
½ Brandy.
Shake well and strain into cocktail glass.

GENE CORRIE COCKTAIL.

½ Hercules. ½ Dry Gin.
Shake well and strain into cocktail glass.

GENE TUNNEY COCKTAIL.

1 Dash Orange Juice.
1 Dash Lemon Juice.
⅓ French Vermouth.
⅔ Plymouth Gin.
Shake well and strain into cocktail glass.

GENEVIÈVE COCKTAIL.
⅓ Hollands Gin.
⅔ Hercules.
Stir well and strain into cocktail glass.

GIBSON COCKTAIL.
½ French Vermouth.
½ Gin.
Shake well and strain into cocktail glass. Squeeze lemon peel on top.

GILROY COCKTAIL.
⅙ Lemon Juice.
⅙ French Vermouth.
⅓ Cherry Brandy.
⅓ Dry Gin.
1 Dash Orange Bitters.
Shake well and strain into cocktail glass.

GIMBLET COCKTAIL.
¼ Lime Juice. ¾ Dry Gin.
Shake well and strain into medium size glass; fill up with soda water.

GIMLET COCKTAIL.
½ Burrough's Plymouth Gin.
½ Rose's Lime Juice Cordial.
Stir, and serve in same glass. Can be iced if desired.

GIN COCKTAIL.
4 Dashes Orange Bitters.
1 Glass Dry Gin.
Shake well and strain into cocktail glass.

COCKTAILS

GIN AND CAPE COCKTAIL.	½ Caperitif. ½ Dry Gin. *Stir well and strain into cocktail glass. Squeeze lemon peel on top.*
GLAD EYE COCKTAIL.	⅓ Peppermint. ⅔ Absinthe. *Shake well and strain into cocktail glass.*
GLOOM CHASER COCKTAIL.	¼ Lemon Juice. ¼ Grenadine. ¼ Grand Marnier. ¼ Curaçao. *Shake well and strain into cocktail glass.*
GOLDEN ERMINE COCKTAIL.	⅛ Italian Vermouth. ⅜ French Vermouth. ½ Dry Gin. *Shake well and strain into cocktail glass.*
THE GOLDEN GATE COCKTAIL.	¾ Orange Ice. ¼ Gin. *Place in shaker and shake—no ice.*
GOLDEN SLIPPER COCKTAIL.	½ Liqueur Glass Yellow Chartreuse. The Yolk of 1 Fresh Egg. ½ Liqueur Glass Eau de Vie de Danzig. *Shake well and strain into cocktail glass.*

COCKTAILS

Fill a large glass with broken ice and place in it 2 glasses of Whisky, 2½ glasses of French Vermouth and half a glass of Raspberry Brandy. Add the juice of half an Orange, a teaspoonful of Orange-flower water, 3 Juniper berries, a bit of Cinnamon and a little Nutmeg.
Stir well with a big silver spoon, pour the mixture, straining it, into a cocktail shaker holding about a pint. Shake and keep for on hour on ice. Serve.

GRACE'S DELIGHT COCKTAIL.
(6 people)

¼ Dry Gin.
¼ Apricot Brandy.
½ Bacardi Rum.
Shake well and strain into cocktail glass.

GRADEAL (SPECIAL) COCKTAIL.

The Juice of ½ Lemon.
1 Tablespoonful Grenadine.
1 Egg. 1 Glass Dry Gin.
Shake well and strain into medium size glass.

GRAND ROYAL CLOVER CLUB COCKTAIL.

¼ French Vermouth.
¼ Italian Vermouth.
½ Swedish Punch.
Shake well and strain into cocktail glass.

GRAND SLAM COCKTAIL.

¼ Grape Juice.
¼ Lemon Juice. ½ Gin.
1 Dash Grenadine.
Shake well and strain into cocktail glass.

THE GRAPE VINE COCKTAIL.

COCKTAILS

GRAPEFRUIT COCKTAIL.
(6 people)

The Juice of 1½ Lemons.
2 Small Spoonsful Grapefruit Jelly.
4 Glasses Gin.
Add Ice and shake.

One may in this Cocktail replace the Grapefruit Jelly by any other Fruit Jelly of distinctive taste.

The following Cocktail, although apparently harmless, is sometimes liable to be snappy. It is a variation of the Grapefruit Cocktail:-

Take three and a half glasses of Gin and the juice of 1½ good-sized Grapefruit. Sugar to taste, plenty of ice. Shake and serve.

GREAT SECRET COCKTAIL.

1 Dash Angostura Bitters.
⅓ Kina Lillet.
⅔ Dry Gin.
Shake well and strain into cocktail glass. Squeeze orange peel on top.

GREENBRIAR COCKTAIL.

1 Dash Peach Bitters.
⅓ French Vermouth.
⅔ Sherry.
1 Sprig Fresh Mint.
Shake well and strain into cocktail glass.

COCKTAILS

⅛ Lemon Juice.
⅛ Kummel.
¼ Green Mint.
½ Dry Gin.
4 Dashes Peach Bitters.
Shake well and strain into
cocktail glass.

GREEN DRAGON COCKTAIL.

⅓ Brandy
⅔ French Vermouth.
2 Dashes Curaçao.
Shake well and strain into
cocktail glass.

GREEN ROOM COCKTAIL.

This Cocktail, a great favourite with mummers, is an excellent " pick-me-up."

1 Dash Jamaica Ginger.
⅓ Ginger Brandy.
⅔ Brandy.
1 Teaspoonful Powdered Sugar.
Shake well and strain into
cocktail glass.

GRENADIER COCKTAIL.

2 Dashes Curaçao.
⅓ Italian Vermouth.
⅔ Dry Gin.
Shake well and strain into
cocktail glass.

GUARD'S COCKTAIL.

½ Italian Vermouth.
½ Plymouth Gin.
Shake well and strain into
cocktail glass.

GYPSY COCKTAIL.

COCKTAILS

We picture the beautiful Lady Cynthia, after imbibing a Corpse Reviver Cocktail.

HAKAM COCKTAIL.
> 1 Dash Orange Bitters.
> 2 Dashes Curaçao.
> ½ Dry Gin.
> ½ Italian Vermouth.
> *Shake well and strain into cocktail glass.*

H. AND H. COCKTAIL.*
> 2 Dashes Curaçao.
> ⅓ Glass Kina Lillet.
> ⅔ Glass Dry Gin.
> *Shake well and strain into cocktail glass. Squeeze orange peel on top.*

* Happier and Happier ? or Hoarser and Hoarser ? or Hazier and Hazier ?

HANKY PANKY COCKTAIL.
> 2 Dashes Fernet Branca.
> ½ Italian Vermouth.
> ½ Dry Gin.
> *Shake well and strain into cocktail glass. Squeeze orange peel on top.*

COCKTAILS

½ Italian Vermouth.
½ Tom Gin.
*Shake well and strain into
cocktail glass.*

**H.P.W.
COCKTAIL.**

1 Dash Angostura Bitters.
1 Teaspoonful Orange Juice.
1 Dash Lemon Juice.
1 Glass Dry Gin.
*Shake well and strain into
cocktail glass.*

**HARROVIAN
COCKTAIL.**

⅓ Gancia Italian Vermouth.
1 Dash Absinthe.   ⅔ Gin.
2 Sprigs of Fresh Mint.
*Shake well and strain into cock-
tail glass. Serve with a stuffed
olive.*

**HARRY'S
COCKTAIL.**

1 Teaspoonful Grenadine.
1 Glass Brandy.
    The Juice of ½ Lemon.
*Shake well and strain into
medium sized wine glass, and fill
balance with Champagne.*

**HARRY'S
PICK-ME-UP
COCKTAIL.**

2 Dashes Angostura Bitters.
1 Dash Syrup.   ½ Brandy.
½ Italian Vermouth.
*Shake well and strain into
cocktail glass.*

**HARVARD
COCKTAIL.**

1 Dash Absinthe.
4 Dashes Grenadine.
⅓ French Vermouth.
⅔ Nicholson's Gin.
Shake well and strain into cocktail glass.

**HASTY
COCKTAIL**

81

COCKTAILS

HAVANA COCKTAIL.

1 Dash Lemon Juice.
¼ Dry Gin.
¼ Swedish Punch.
½ Apricot Brandy.
Shake well and strain into cocktail glass.

HAWAIIAN COCKTAIL.

4 Parts Gin.
2 Parts Orange Juice.
1 Part Curaçao (or any other of the Orange Liqueurs).
Shake well and strain into cocktail glass.

HEALTH COCKTAIL.

⅓ Brandy. ⅔ Hercules.
Stir slightly in ice and strain. Any desired spirit can be used instead of Brandy.

HELL COCKTAIL. (6 people)

Shake 3 glasses of Cognac and 3 glasses of Green Crème de Menthe. Serve with a pinch of red pepper on each glass.

HESITATION COCKTAIL.

1 Dash Lemon Juice.
¼ Canadian Club Whisky.
¾ Swedish Punch.
Shake well and strain into cocktail glass.

HONEY-MOON COCKTAIL.

The Juice of ½ Lemon.*
3 Dashes Curaçao.
½ Bénédictine.
½ Apple Brandy.
Shake well and strain into cocktail glass.
* Some sensitive bartenders think it more tactful to substitute orange juice.

COCKTAILS

2 Dashes Orange Bitters.
⅓ French Vermouth.
⅔ Plymouth Gin.
*Shake well and strain into cock-
tail glass.   Squeeze lemon peel
on top.*

HOFFMAN
HOUSE
COCKTAIL.

The Juice of ¼ Lemon.
1 Slice Pineapple.
⅓ French Vermouth.
⅔ Dry Gin.
4 Dashes Maraschino.
*Shake well and strain into
cocktail glass.*

HOLLAND
HOUSE
COCKTAIL.

---

1 Slice Orange.   ⅔ Dry Gin.
⅓ Italian Vermouth.
*Shake well and strain into
cocktail glass.*

HOMESTEAD
COCKTAIL.

Although this delightful drink is nowadays known
as a Cocktail, it was known in the old homesteads
of the Southern States long before the name
Cocktail was coined.

---

1 Dash Angostura Bitters.
1 Dash Orange Juice.
1 Dash Pineapple Juice.
1 Dash Lemon Juice.
1 Glass Dry Gin.
A little Powdered Sugar.
*Shake well and strain into
cocktail glass.*

HONOLULU
COCKTAIL.
(No. 1.)

⅓ Maraschino.   ⅓ Gin.
⅓ Bénédictine.
*Shake well and strain into
cocktail glass.*

HONOLULU
COCKTAIL.
(No. 2.)

"HOOP LA!" COCKTAIL.
¼ Lemon Juice.
¼ Kina Lillet.
¼ Cointreau. ¼ Brandy.
Shake well and strain into cocktail glass.

"HOOTS MON" COCKTAIL.
¼ Kina Lillet.
¼ Italian Vermouth.
½ Scotch Whisky.
Stir well and strain into cocktail glass.

HOP TOAD COCKTAIL.
¼ Lemon Juice.
¾ Apricot Brandy.
Shake well and strain into cocktail glass.

HOT DECK COCKTAIL.
1 Dash Jamaica Ginger.
¼ Italian Vermouth.
¾ Canadian Club Whisky.
Shake well and strain into cocktail glass.

HOULA-HOULA COCKTAIL.
1 Dash Curaçao.
⅓ Orange Juice.
⅔ Dry Gin.
Shake well and strain into cocktail glass.

COCKTAILS

⅙ Orange Juice.
⅙ Lemon Juice.
⅔ Swedish Punch.
2 Dashes Grenadine.
Shake well and strain into cocktail glass.

THE HUNDRED PER CENT COCKTAIL.

⅓ Whisky. ⅓ Gin.
⅓ Crème de Menthe.
The Juice of 2 Lemons.
Shake well and strain into cocktail glass.

THE HURRICANE COCKTAIL.

In a wineglass place one lump of Ice, 3 dashes of Fernet Branca, 3 dashes of Curaçao, one liqueur glass of Brandy, fill remainder with Champagne.
Stir and squeeze lemon peel on top.

I.B.F. PICK-ME-UP COCKTAIL.

The Yolk of 1 Egg.
1 Port-wine Glass Milk.
¼ Orange Curaçao.
¾ Brandy.
Shake well and strain into medium size glass, with nutmeg on top.

ICHBIEN COCKTAIL.

3 Dashes Maraschino.
⅓ Italian Vermouth.
⅔ Dry Gin.
1 Tablespoonful Grapefruit Juice.
Shake well and strain into cocktail glass. Serve small nut in glass.

IDEAL COCKTAIL.

COCKTAILS

IMPERIAL COCKTAIL.
1 Dash Maraschino.
1 Dash Angostura Bitters.
½ French Vermouth.
½ Dry Gin.
Stir well and serve with olive.

INCA COCKTAIL.
1 Dash Orgeat Syrup.
1 Dash Orange Bitters.
¼ Gin. ¼ Sherry.
¼ French Vermouth.
¼ Italian Vermouth.
Shake well and strain into cocktail glass.

INCOME TAX COCKTAIL.
1 Dash Angostura Bitters.
The Juice of ¼ Orange.
¼ French Vermouth.
¼ Italian Vermouth.
½ Dry Gin.
Shake well and strain into cocktail glass.

INK STREET COCKTAIL.
⅓ Canadian Club Whisky.
⅓ Orange Juice.
⅓ Lemon Juice.
Shake well, then strain into cocktail glass.

Picture of Conscientious Gentleman making pathetic but laudable endeavour to appreciate the æsthetic subtlety of a park masterpiece by a famous sculptor of the Period.

COCKTAILS

IRISH COCKTAIL.

2 Dashes Absinthe.
2 Dashes Curaçao.
1 Dash Maraschino.
1 Dash Angostura Bitters.
½ Glass Irish Whisky.

Shake well and strain into cocktail glass. Add olive and squeeze orange peel on top.

JABBERWOCK COCKTAIL.*

2 Dashes Orange Bitters.
⅓ Dry Gin.   ⅓ Dry Sherry.
⅓ Caperitif.

Stir well and strain into cocktail glass. Squeeze lemon peel on top.

* This will made you gyre and gimble in the wabe until brillig all right, all right.

COCKTAILS

JACK KEARNS COCKTAIL. (No. 1.)	1 Dash Lemon Juice. 1 Dash Syrup. ¼ Bacardi Rum. ¾ Dry Gin. *Shake well and strain into cocktail glass.*
JACK KEARNS COCKTAIL. (No. 2.)	¼ Bacardi Rum. 1 Dash Lemon Juice. 1 Dash Syrup. ¾ Dry Gin. *Shake well and strain into cocktail glass.*
JACK PINE COCKTAIL.	The Juice of ¼ Orange. 1 Slice Pineapple. ¾ Dry Gin. ¼ French Vermouth. *Shake well and strain into cocktail glass.*
JACK ROSE COCKTAIL.	The Juice of ½ Lemon or 1 Lime. ¼ Grenadine. ¾ Applejack or Calvados.

Shake well and strain into cocktail glass.

JACKSON COCKTAIL.	2 Dashes Orange Bitters. ½ Orange Gin. ½ Dubonnet.

Stir well and strain into cocktail glass.

JACK WITHERS COCKTAIL.	The Juice of ½ Orange. ⅓ French Vermouth. ⅓ Italian Vermouth. ⅓ Dry Gin.

Shake well and strain into cocktail glass.

COCKTAILS

2 Glasses Green Chartreuse.
2 Glasses Italian Vermouth.
2 Glasses Gin.
½ Dessertspoonful Orange
    Bitters.
*Shake thoroughly and serve with
a cherry, squeezing lemon peel on
top.*

**JEWEL
COCKTAIL.**
(6 people)

A medium-dry, fast-working cocktail.

1 Dash Absinthe.
⅔ Dry Gin.
⅓ Italian Vermouth.
*Shake well and strain into cock-
tail glass. Squeeze lemon peel
on top.*

**JEYPLAK
COCKTAIL.**

3 Dashes Dubonnet.
⅓ Kina Lillet. ⅔ Dry Gin.
*Shake well and strain into cock-
tail glass. Squeeze orange peel
on top.*

**JIMMY BLANC
COCKTAIL.**

4 Dashes Orange Bitters.
½ Glass Caperitif.
½ Glass Bacardi Rum.
*Stir well and strain into cocktail
glass. Squeeze lemon peel on
top.*

**JOBURG
COCKTAIL.**

1 Dash Orange Bitters.
1 Dash Angostura Bitters.
2 Dashes Crème de Noyau.
4 Dashes Lemon Juice.
¾ Glass Dry Gin.
*Shake well and strain into cock-
tail glass.*

**JOCKEY
CLUB
COCKTAIL.**

COCKTAILS

JOHNNIE MACK COCKTAIL.

3 Dashes Absinthe.
⅓ Orange Curaçao.
⅔ Sloe Gin.
Shake well and strain into cocktail glass.

JOHN WOOD COCKTAIL.

2 Parts Irish Whisky.
4 Parts Italian Vermouth.
2 Parts Lemon Juice.
1 Part Kummel.
1 Dash Angostura Bitters.
Shake well and strain into cocktail glass.

J.O.S. COCKTAIL.

1 Dash Orange Bitters.
1 Dash Lemon Juice or Lime Juice.
1 Dash Brandy.
⅓ Italian Vermouth.
⅓ French Vermouth.
⅓ Dry Gin.
Shake well and strain into cocktail glass. Squeeze lemon peel on top.

JOURNALIST COCKTAIL.

2 Dashes Lemon Juice.
2 Dashes Curaçao.
1 Dash Angostura Bitters.
⅙ French Vermouth.
⅙ Italian Vermouth.
⅔ Gordon's Dry Gin.
Shake well and strain into cocktail glass.

COCKTAILS

⅓ Gin. ⅓ Bacardi Rum.
⅓ Lemon Juice.
  Powdered Sugar.
1 Dash of Grenadine.
*Shake well and strain into
  cocktail glass.*

THE JUDGE,
JR.
COCKTAIL.

⅓ Peach Brandy. ⅓ Gin.
⅓ French Vermouth.
1 Dash of Lime.
*Shake well and strain into
  cocktail glass.*

THE
JUDGETTE
COCKTAIL.

1 Teaspoonful Orange Juice.
1 Teaspoonful Parfait
  Amour Liqueur.
⅓ French Vermouth.
⅔ Dry Gin.
*Shake well and strain into
  cocktail glass.*

JUPITER
COCKTAIL.

1 Dash Apricot Brandy.
1 Dash Lemon Juice.
¼ Kirsch. ¾ Dry Gin.
*Shake well and strain into
  cocktail glass.*

K.C.B.
COCKTAIL.

COCKTAILS

KICKER COCKTAIL.

2 Dashes Italian Vermouth.
1/3 Calvados.
2/3 Bacardi Rum.
Shake well and strain into cocktail glass.

KINA COCKTAIL.

1/4 Kina Lillet. 1/2 Dry Gin.
1/4 Italian Vermouth.
Shake well and strain into cocktail glass.

KING COLE COCKTAIL.

1 Glass Rye or Canadian Club Whisky.
2 Dashes Syrup.
1 Dash Fernet Branca.
1 Lump of Ice.
Stir well and decorate with slices of orange and pineapple.

KINGSTON COCKTAIL. (6 people)

3 Glasses Jamaica Rum.
1 1/2 Glasses Kummel.
1 1/2 Glasses Orange Juice.
1 Dash Pimento Dram.
Shake carefully and serve whilst frothing.

The unique taste of this cocktail is due to Kummel mixed with a liqueur known as Pimento Dram (a Jamaican liqueur), without which it would lose all its distinction.

KNICKER-BOCKER COCKTAIL.

1 Dash Italian Vermouth.
1/3 French Vermouth.
2/3 Dry Gin.
Shake well and strain into cocktail glass. Squeeze lemon peel on top.

COCKTAILS

1 Teaspoonful Raspberry Syrup.
1 Teaspoonful Lemon Juice.
1 Teaspoonful Orange Juice.
1 Chunk of Pineapple.
$2/3$ Rum.
2 Dashes of Curaçao.

KNICKER-BOCKER SPECIAL COCKTAIL.

1 Teaspoonful White Crème de Menthe.
$1/3$ Absinthe. $1/3$ Dry Gin.
$1/3$ French Vermouth.
Shake well and strain into cocktail glass.

KNOCK OUT COCKTAIL.

$1/3$ Dry Gin. $2/3$ Kola Tonic.
2 Dashes Orange Bitters.
Shake well and strain into cocktail glass.

KOLA TONIC COCKTAIL.

1 Dash Absinthe.
$1/8$ Italian Vermouth.
$1/4$ French Vermouth.
$5/8$ Dry Gin.
Shake well and strain into cocktail glass. Squeeze orange peel on top.

KUP'S INDISPENS-ABLE COCKTAIL

2 Dashes Absinthe.
2 Dashes Anisette.
2 Dashes Angostura Bitters.
1 Glass of Canadian Club Whisky.
Stir well and put small piece of pineapple in glass.

LADIES' COCKTAIL.

COCKTAILS

LASKY COCKTAIL.

⅓ Grape Juice.
⅓ Swedish Punch. ⅓ Dry Gin
*Shake well and strain into
    cocktail glass.*

LAWHILL COCKTAIL.

1 Dash Absinthe.
1 Dash Maraschino.
1 Dash Angostura Bitters.
⅓ French Vermouth.
⅔ Canadian Club Whisky.
*Shake well and strain into
    cocktail glass.*

LEAP-FROG COCKTAIL.

1 Lump of Ice.
    The Juice of ½ Lemon.
1 Glass Gin.
1 Split of Ginger Ale.
Serve in long tumbler.

LEAP YEAR COCKTAIL.

1 Dash Lemon Juice.
⅔ Gin. ⅙ Grand Marnier.
⅙ Italian Vermouth.
*Shake well and serve in cocktail
    glass. Squeeze lemon peel on top.*

This Cocktail was created by Harry Craddock, for the Leap Year celebrations at the Savoy Hotel, London, on February 29th, 1928. It is said to have been responsible for more proposals than any other cocktail that has ever been mixed.

LEAVE IT TO ME COCKTAIL. (No. 1.)

1 Dash Lemon Juice.
¼ Apricot Brandy.
¼ French Vermouth.
1 Dash Grenadine.
½ Plymouth Gin.
*Shake well and strain into
    cocktail glass.*

COCKTAILS

1 Teaspoonful Raspberry Syrup.
1 Teaspoonful Lemon Juice.
1 Dash Maraschino.
¾ Glass Dry Gin.
Shake well and strain into cocktail glass.

LEAVE IT TO ME COCKTAIL. (No. 2.)

1 Glass Scotch Whisky.
1 bottle Lemonade.

LEMON PIE COCKTAIL.

1 Glass Scotch Whisky.
1 Glass Beer as a chaser.

"L.G." COCKTAIL.

1 Dash Syrup.
⅓ Bacardi Rum.
⅔ Apple Jack.
Shake well and strain into cocktail glass.

LIBERTY COCKTAIL.

1 Dash Lemon Juice.
⅓ Dry Gin. ⅓ Kina Lillet.
⅓ Crème de Noyau.
Shake well and strain into cocktail glass.

LILY COCKTAIL.

CHARLIE LINDBERGH COCKTAIL.	2 Dashes Orange Juice. 2 Dashes Pricota. ½ Kina Lillet. ½ Plymouth Gin. *Shake well and serve in cocktail glass. Squeeze lemon peel on top.*
LINSTEAD COCKTAIL. (6 people)	3 Glasses Whisky. 3 Glasses Sweetened Pineapple Juice. Finish off before shaking with a dash of Absinthe Bitters. *Shake and serve, squeezing a little lemon peel on top of each glass.*
LITTLE DEVIL COCKTAIL.	⅙ Lemon Juice. ⅙ Cointreau. ⅓ Bacardi Rum. ⅓ Dry Gin. *Shake well and strain into cocktail glass.*
LITTLE PRINCESS COCKTAIL.	½ Italian Vermouth. ½ Bacardi Rum. *Shake well and strain into cocktail glass.*

COCKTAILS

2 Dashes Orange Bitters.
2 Dashes Syrup.
2 Dashes Absinthe.
⅓ Dry Gin.
*Shake well and strain into
cocktail glass.*

**LONDON
COCKTAIL.**

1 Lump of Ice.
1 Glass Dry Gin.
The Juice of ½ Lemon.
1 Split of Ginger Ale.
Use long tumbler.

**LONDON
BUCK
COCKTAIL.**

2 Dashes Orange Bitters.
⅓ Italian Vermouth.
⅓ French Vermouth.
⅓ Dry Gin.
*Shake well and strain into
cocktail glass.*

**LONE
TREE
COCKTAIL.**

⅛ Italian Vermouth.
⅛ Cointreau. ⅝ Dry Gin.
⅛ Maraschino.
*Shake well and strain into
cocktail glass.*

**LORD
SUFFOLK.
COCKTAIL.**

The Juice of 1 Lemon.
4 Hookers Whisky.
4 Teaspoonsful Sugar
1 Egg.
1 Dash Italian Vermouth.
*Shake well and strain into
cocktail glass.*

**THE LOS
ANGELES
COCKTAIL.
(4 people)**

97

COCKTAILS

LOUD SPEAKER COCKTAIL.

⅛ Lemon Juice.
⅛ Cointreau.
³⁄₈ Dry Gin.
³⁄₈ Brandy.
Shake well and strain into cocktail glass

This it is that gives to Radio Announcers their peculiar enunciation. Three of them will produce oscillation, and after five it is possible to reach the osculation stage.

LUIGI COCKTAIL.

1 Teaspoonful Grenadine.
1 Dash Cointreau.
The Juice of ½ Tangerine.
½ Dry Gin.
½ French Vermouth.
Shake well and strain into cocktail glass.

LUTKINS SPECIAL COCKTAIL.

2 Dashes Orange Juice.
2 Dashes Apricot Brandy.
½ French Vermouth.
½ Dry Gin.
Shake well and strain into cocktail glass.

MACARONI COCKTAIL.

⅓ Italian Vermouth.
⅔ Absinthe.
Shake well and strain into cocktail glass.

McCLELLAND COCKTAIL.

1 Dash Absinthe.
⅓ Curaçao.
⅔ Sloe Gin.
Shake well and strain into cocktail glass.

COCKTAILS

¼ Lemon Juice. ¼ Cream.
½ Gin.
1 Dash Grenadine.
Shake well and strain into
cocktail glass.

THE
MAGNOLIA
BLOSSOM
COCKTAIL.

⅙ Cointreau.
⅙ Bacardi Rum.
⅔ Dry Gin.
Shake well and strain into
cocktail glass.

MAH-JONGG
COCKTAIL.

1 Dash Lemon Juice.
4 Dashes Orange Curaçao.
4 Dashes Grenadine.
1 Glass Dry Gin.
Shake well and strain into
cocktail glass.

MAIDEN'S
BLUSH
COCKTAIL.
(No. 1.)

⅓ Absinthe. ⅔ Dry Gin
1 Teaspoonful Grenadine.
Shake well and strain into
cocktail glass.

MAIDEN'S
BLUSH
COCKTAIL.
(No. 2.)

⅛ Orange Juice.
⅛ Lemon Juice.
⅜ Cointreau. ⅜ Dry Gin.
Shake well and strain into
cocktail glass.

MAIDEN'S
PRAYER
COCKTAIL.
(No. 1.)

⅓ Kina Lillet. ⅓ Dry Gin.
⅙ Calvados. ⅙ Pricota.
Shake well and strain into
cocktail glass.

MAIDEN'S
PRAYER
COCKTAIL.
(No. 2.)

* On the principle that if at first you don't
succeed, cry, cry again.

COCKTAILS

THE MAMIE TAYLOR COCKTAIL.

1 Hooker Whisky.
The Juice of 2 Limes.
Fill tall glass with Ginger Ale.

MANHATTAN COCKTAIL. (No. 1.)

Use small Bar glass.
2 Dashes Curacao or Maraschino.
1 Pony Rye Whisky.
1 Wineglass Vermouth (Mixed).
3 Dashes Angostura Bitters.
2 Small Lumps of Ice.
Shake up well, and strain into a claret glass. Put a quarter of a slice of lemon in the glass and serve. If preferred very sweet add two dashes of gum syrup.

MANHATTAN COCKTAIL. (No. 2.)

1 Dash Angostura Bitters.
⅔ Canadian Club Whisky.
⅓ Ballor Italian Vermouth.
Shake well, strain into cocktail glass, with cherry.
(Named after the island on which New York City Stands.)

COCKTAILS

½ Italian Vermouth.
½ Rye or Canadian Club
    Whisky.
Stir well and strain into
*   cocktail glass.*

**MANHATTAN
COCKTAIL.**
(SWEET).

¼ French Vermouth.
¼ Italian Vermouth.
½ Rye or Canadian Club
    Whisky.
Stir well and strain into
*   cocktail glass.*

**MANHATTAN
COCKTAIL.**
(DRY).

The Juice of 1 Lemon.
2 Dashes Curaçao.
½ Gin. ½ Caperitif.
Shake well and strain into
*   port wine glass.*

**MANYANN
COCKTAIL.**

⅓ Bacardi Rum.
⅓ French Vermouth.
⅓ Italian Vermouth.
1 Dash Kirsch.
    The Juice of ½ Lemon.
    The Juice of ⅓ Lime.
    A little sugar dissolved in
       soda-water.
Shake well and serve in cocktail
*   glass.*

**MARAGATO
COCKTAIL.
(SPECIAL).**

1 Dash Orange Bitters.
⅓ French Vermouth.
⅔ Dry Gin.
Shake well and strain into cock-
tail glass. Twist orange peel on
*   top.*

**MARGUERITE
COCKTAIL.**

COCKTAILS

MARMALADE COCKTAIL.
(6 people)

By its bitter-sweet taste this cocktail is especially suited to be a luncheon aperitif. Place the following mixture in the shaker :

2 Dessertspoonsful Orange Marmalade.
The Juice of 1 big or 2 small Lemons.
4 Glasses Gin.

Shake carefully and pour out, squeezing a piece of orange rind into each glass.

MARNY COCKTAIL.

⅓ Grand Marnier.
⅔ Dry Gin.
Shake well and strain into cocktail glass.

MARTINEZ COCKTAIL.
(6 people)

Pour into the shaker 3 glasses of Gin, 3 of French Vermouth, add a dessertspoonful of Orange Bitters and 2 of Curaçao or Maraschino. *Shake and serve with a cherry and a piece of lemon rind.*

MARTINI
(DRY)
COCKTAIL.

⅓ French Vermouth.
⅔ Dry Gin.
Shake well and strain into cocktail glass.

MARTINI
(MEDIUM)
COCKTAIL.

¼ French Vermouth.
¼ Italian Vermouth.
½ Dry Gin.
Shake well and strain into cocktail glass.

COCKTAILS

⅓ Italian Vermouth.
⅔ London Gin.
*Shake well and strain into
cocktail glass.*

MARTINI
(SWEET)
COCKTAIL.

4 Glasses of Gin.
1½ Glasses Italian Vermouth.
⅓ Glass Orange-flower
Water.
*Before shaking, add a dash of
Absinthe and one or two dashes
of Angostura Bitters.*

MARTINI
(SPECIAL)
COCKTAIL.
(6 people)

¾ Jamaica Rum.
⅛ Sirop-de-Citron.
⅛ Grenadine.
*Shake well and strain into
cocktail glass.*

THE MARVEL
COCKTAIL.

½ Bacardi Rum.
½ Pineapple Juice.
1 Teaspoonful Grenadine.
6 Drops Maraschino.

MARY
PICKFORD
COCKTAIL.

1 Dash Absinthe.
The Juice of ¼ Orange.
¼ Italian Vermouth.
¼ French Vermouth.
½ Dry Gin.
*Shake well and strain into
cocktail glass.*

MAURICE
COCKTAIL.

1 Dash Clove Syrup.
¼ Apricot Brandy.
¼ Orange Juice. ½ Dry Gin.
*Shake well and strain into
cocktail glass.*

MAYFAIR
COCKTAIL.

COCKTAILS

MELBA COCKTAIL.
2 Dashes Grenadine.
2 Dashes Absinthe.
The Juice of ¼ Lemon or ½ Lime.
½ Glass Bacardi Rum.
½ Glass Swedish Punch.
Shake well and strain into cocktail glass.

MELON COCKTAIL.
⅛ Lemon Juice.
⅜ Maraschino. ½ Gin.
Shake well and strain into cocktail glass.

MERRY WIDOW COCKTAIL.
2 Dashes Absinthe.
2 Dashes Angostura Bitters.
2 Dashes Bénédictine.
½ French Vermouth.
½ Dry Gin.
Stir well and strain into cocktail glass. Twist lemon peel on top.

MICKIE WALKER COCKTAIL.
1 Dash Grenadine.
1 Dash Lemon Juice.
¼ Italian Vermouth.
¾ Scotch Whisky.
Shake well and strain into cocktail glass.

COCKTAILS

2 Dashes Angostura Bitters.
2 Dashes Crème de Noyau.
2 Dashes Orgeat Syrup.
2 Dashes Curaçao.
½ Glass Brandy.
Shake well and strain into
cocktail glass.

MIKADO COCKTAIL.

The Juice of 1 Lime.
1 Dash Grenadine.
⅓ Sloe Gin.
⅓ Apricot Brandy.
⅓ Jamaica Rum.
Shake well and strain into
cocktail glass.

MILLIONAIRE COCKTAIL. (No. 1.)

1 Dash Anisette.
The White of 1 Egg.
⅓ Absinthe. ⅔ Dry Gin.
Shake well and strain into
cocktail glass.

MILLIONAIRE COCKTAIL. (No. 2.)

Tablespoonful Pineapple
Juice.
Teaspoonful Grenadine.
The White of 1 Egg.
⅓ Italian Vermouth.
⅔ Plymouth Gin.
Shake well and strain into
medium size glass.

MILLION DOLLAR COCKTAIL.

The Juice of ¼ Orange.
¼ French Vermouth.
¼ Italian Vermouth.
½ Dry Gin. 1 Dash Absinthe.
Shake well and strain into
cocktail glass.

MINNEHAHA COCKTAIL.

COCKTAILS

MINT COCKTAIL.
(6 people)

Soak a few sprigs of fresh mint for two hours in a glass and a half of White Wine. Add half a glass of Crème de Menthe, 2 glasses of Gin and 1 ½ glasses of White Wine. Ice and shake thoroughly.
Serve with a sprig of mint tastefully arranged in each glass.

MISSISSIPPI MULE COCKTAIL.

⅔ Dry Gin. ⅙ Lemon Juice. ⅙ Crème de Cassis.
Shake well and strain into cocktail glass.

Mr. MANHATTAN COCKTAIL.

Crush one lump of sugar in a little water.
Then crush four leaves of fresh green mint, and add—
　1 Dash Lemon Juice.
　4 Dashes Orange Juice.
　1 Glass Gin.
Shake well and strain into cocktail glass.

Picture of Portly Butler of Proud Lineage, expressing utter consternation upon inadvertently opening the door to quite a few
　　Gay
　　　Young
　　　　Things.

COCKTAILS

1 Dash Orange Bitters.
2 Dashes Jamaica Rum.
1 Dash Absinthe.
2 Dashes Lemon Juice.
1 Glass Scotch Whisky.
*Shake well and strain into
cocktail glass.*

MODERN
COCKTAIL
(No. 1.)

1 Dash Orange Bitters.
1 Dash Absinthe.
1 Dash Grenadine.
⅓ Scotch Whisky.
⅔ Sloe Gin.
*Shake well and strain into
cocktail glass.*

MODERN
COCKTAIL.
(No. 2.)

¼ French Vermouth.
¼ Caperitif. ½ Dry Gin.
*Stir well and strain into
cocktail glass.*

MODDER
RIVER
COCKTAIL.

2 Glasses Gin.
2 Glasses Sloe Gin.
2 Glasses French Vermouth.
Add a few drops of Orange
Bitters and sugar to taste.
Shake and serve in cocktail glasses.

MOLL
COCKTAIL.
(6 people)

3 Dashes Absinthe.
3 Dashes Grenadine.
⅓ Orange Juice.
⅔ Dry Gin.
*Shake well and strain into
cocktail glass.*

MONKEY
GLAND
COCKTAIL.

COCKTAILS

MONTE CARLO IMPERIAL COCKTAIL.

½ Dry Gin.
¼ Lemon Juice.
¼ White Crème de Menthe.
Shake well and strain into medium-size glass and fill up with Champagne.

MONTPELIER COCKTAIL.

⅓ French Vermouth.
⅔ Dry Gin.
Shake well and strain into cocktail glass. Add a pickled pearl onion.

MOONLIGHT COCKTAIL. (6 peope)

1½ Glasses Grape-fruit Juice.
2 Glasses Gin.
½ Glass Kirsch.
2 Glasses White Wine.
Add ice and shake thoroughly. Serve by placing in each glass a thin shaving of lemon peel.

A very dry cocktail.

MOON-RAKER COCKTAIL. (6 people)

Pour into the shaker 2 glasses of Brandy, 2 of Quinquina and 2 of Peach Brandy. Add 3 dashes of Absinthe, shake vigorously and serve.

MOONSHINE COCKTAIL. (6 people)

3 Glasses Gin.
2 Glasses French Vermouth.
1 Glass Maraschino.
Before shaking add a drop of Absinthe Bitters.

COCKTAILS

2 Dashes Curaçao.
2 Dashes Maraschino.
2 Dashes Orange Bitters.
2 Dashes Absinthe.
½ Brandy.
½ French Vermouth.
*Shake well and strain into cock-
tail glass. Add a cherry and
squeeze lemon peel on top.*

**MORNING
COCKTAIL.**

3 Dashes Gomme Syrup.
2 Dashes Curaçao.
2 Dashes Bitters.
1 Dash Absinthe.
1 Liqueur Glass Brandy.
1 Liqueur Glass Whisky.
1 Piece Lemon Peel, twisted
        to express the oil.
Two Small Pieces of Ice.
*Stir thoroughly and remove the
ice. Fill the glass with seltzer
water or plain soda, and stir
with a teaspoon having a little
sugar in it.*

**MORNING
GLORY
COCKTAIL.**

3 Dashes Grenadine.
½ Apricot Brandy.
¼ Orange Gin.
¼ Lemon Juice.
*Shake well and strain into
        cocktail glass.*

**MOULIN
ROUGE
COCKTAIL.**

The White of 1 Egg.
⅙ Lemon Juice.
⅙ French Vermouth.
⅙ Italian Vermouth.
½ Canadian Club Whisky.
Shake well and strain into medium-size glass.

**MOUNTAIN
COCKTAIL.**

COCKTAILS

THE MULE'S
HIND LEG
COCKTAIL.

⅕ Gin.   ⅕ Bénédictine.
⅕ Applejack.
⅕ Maple Syrup.
⅕ Apricot Brandy.
*Shake well and strain into
cocktail glass.*

NAPOLEON
COCKTAIL.

1 Dash Fernet Branca.
1 Dash Curaçao.
1 Dash Dubonnet.
1 Glass Dry Gin.
*Shake well and strain into cock-
tail glass.   Squeeze lemon peel
on top.*

THE
NEVADA
COCKTAIL.

1 Hooker of Bacardi Rum.
  The Juice of ½ Grape
    Fruit.
  The Juice of 1 Lime.
  Powdered Sugar.
1 Dash Bitters.
*Shake well and strain into
cocktail glass.*

NEWBURY
COCKTAIL.

1 Piece Lemon Peel.
1 Piece Orange Peel.
3 Dashes Curacao.
½ Italian Vermouth.
½ Dry Gin.
*Shake well and strain into
cocktail glass.*

NEW LIFE
COCKTAIL.

¼ Hercules.
¼ Bacardi Rum.
½ Cointreau.
*Shake well and strain into
cocktail glass.*

COCKTAILS

1 Dash Orange Bitters.
¼ French Vermouth.
¼ Italian Vermouth.
½ Canadian Club Whisky.
Shake well and strain into cocktail glass. Squeeze lemon peel on top.

NEW 1920 COCKTAIL.

1 Dash Angostura Bitters.
¼ Cointreau.
¾ Brandy.
Shake well and strain into cocktail glass.

NEWTON'S SPECIAL COCKTAIL.

1 Lump Sugar.
The Juice of ½ Lime or ¼ Lemon.
2 Dashes Grenadine.
1 Piece Orange Peel.
1 Glass Canadian Club Whisky.
Shake well and strain into cocktail glass.

NEW YORK COCKTAIL.

COCKTAILS

NICK'S OWN COCKTAIL.

1 Dash Angostura Bitters.
1 Dash Absinthe.
½ Italian Vermouth.
½ Brandy.
Shake well and strain into cocktail glass. Add cherry and squeeze lemon peel on top.

NICOLASKI COCKTAIL.

⅔ Brandy.
1 Slice Lemon with a little castor sugar spread over it.
Drink Brandy through the prepared lemon.

NIGHT CAP COCKTAIL.

The Yolk of 1 Egg.
⅓ Anisette.
⅓ Curaçao.
⅓ Brandy.
Shake well and strain into cocktail glass.

NINE-PICK COCKTAIL.

⅔ Absinthe. ⅓ Gin.
1 Dash Angostura Bitters.
1 Dash Orange Bitters.
1 Dash Syrup.
Shake well and strain into cocktail glass.

NINETEEN COCKTAIL.

1 Dash Absinthe.
⅙ Dry Gin. ⅙ Kirsch.
⅔ French Vermouth.
4 Dashes Syrup.
Shake well and strain into cocktail glass.

COCKTAILS

1 Teaspoonful Groseille
    Syrup.
1/6 Pernod Kirsch.
1/6 Crystal Gin.
2/3 French Vermouth.
1 Dash Absinthe.
Shake well and strain into
    cocktail glass.

**NINETEEN-
TWENTY
COCKTAIL.**

2/3 Pernod Absinthe. 1/3 Gin.
1 Dash Angostura Bitters.
1 Dash Orange Bitters.
1 Dash Gomme Syrup.
*Shake well, strain into medium
size wine-glass, and fill balance
    with soda water.*

**NINETEEN-
TWENTY
PICK-ME-UP
COCKTAIL.**

Take one nooker of Gin,
place in it an olive, then deposit the glass carefully in
the bottom of an ordinary
tumbler. Fill the said tumbler
with Water, Ginger Ale, or
What Have You, until almost
to the top of the small glass,
then down the whole thing
quickly.

**THE
NOSE-DIVE
COCKTAIL.**

That is, everything but the small glass.

This Cocktail is very well known among
pilots on American Flying Fields.

1/4 Glass Lemon Juice.
1/4 Glass Kina Lillet.
1/4 Glass Cointreau.
1/4 Glass Brandy.
*Shake well and strain into
    cocktail glass.*

**ODD
McINTYRE
COCKTAIL.**

OH,
HENRY !
COCKTAIL.

⅓ Bénédictine.
⅓ Whisky.
⅓ Ginger Ale.
Stir well and serve.

OLD
ETONIAN
COCKTAIL.

2 Dashes Orange Bitters.
2 Dashes Crème de Noyau.
½ London Gin.
½ Kina Lillet.
Shake well and strain into cocktail glass. Squeeze orange peel on top.

OLD
FASHIONED
COCKTAIL.

1 Lump Sugar.
2 Dashes Angostura Bitters.
1 Glass Rye or Canadian Club Whisky.
Crush sugar and bitters together, add lump of ice, decorate with twist of lemon peel and slice of orange using medium size glass, and stir well. This Cocktail can be made with Brandy, Gin, Rum, etc., instead of Rye Whisky.

COCKTAILS

⅓ Canadian Club Whisky.
⅓ French Vermouth.
⅓ Campari.
*Shake well and strain into
    cocktail glass.*

**"OLD PAL"
COCKTAIL.**

2 Dashes Syrup.
2 Dashes Orange Bitters.
3 Dashes Absinthe.
⅔ Glass Plymouth Gin.
*Shake well and strain into cock-
tail glass with olive and squeeze
    lemon peel on top.*

**OLIVETTE
COCKTAIL.**

⅓ Orange Juice.
⅓ Curaçao.
⅓ Brandy.
*Shake well and strain into
    cocktail glass.*

**OLYMPIC
COCKTAIL.**

1 Dash Orange Juice.
⅓ French Vermouth.
⅓ Italian Vermouth.
⅓ Plymouth Gin.
*Shake well and strain into Port
Wine glass.   Squeeze lemon
peel on top.   Frost edge of glass
    with castor sugar.*

**ONE
EXCITING
NIGHT
COCKTAIL.**

1 Dash Angostura Bitters.
½ Caperitif.
½ Calvados.
*Shake well and strain into
    cocktail glass.*

**OOM PAUL
COCKTAIL.**

COCKTAILS

OPAL COCKTAIL.
(6 people)

3 Glasses Gin.
2 Glasses Orange Juice.
1 Glass of Cointreau.
A little Sugar.
Add a little Orange-flower water.
Shake and serve.

OPENING COCKTAIL.

¼ Grenadine.
¼ Italian Vermouth.
½ Canadian Club Whisky.
Shake well and strain into
cocktail glass.

OPERA COCKTAIL.

⅙ Maraschino.
⅙ Dubonnet.
⅔ Dry Gin.
Shake well and strain into cock-
tail glass. Squeeze orange peel
on top.

ORANGE COCKTAIL.
(6 people)

Take a glass and a half of
fresh orange juice, a dessertspoonful of Orange Bitters, 3
glasses of Gin, a dessertspoonful of sugar syrup (or a
heaped spoonful of powdered
sugar) and nearly a glass of
French Vermouth. Place the
shaker on ice for half an
hour, and then shake with 2
or 3 large lumps of ice, so as
not to produce too much
water. Squeeze a piece of
orange peel over each glass
and serve.

COCKTAILS

¼ Italian Vermouth.
¼ Cointreau. ½ Dry Gin.
Shake well and strain into cocktail glass and add a cherry.

ORANGE BLOOM COCKTAIL.

½ Orange Juice. ½ Dry Gin.
Shake well and strain into cocktail glass.

ORANGE BLOSSOM COCKTAIL.

2½ Glasses of Gin.
2 Glasses of French Vermouth.
1 Glass of Italian Vermouth.
Steep in this mixture the finely-grated rind of 1 orange (carefully removing all the white pith). Let it soak for one or two hours. Then add ice and shake. Rinse out the glasses with Orange Bitters.

ORANGE MARTINI COCKTAIL.
(6 people)

½ Rye Whisky.
¼ Italian Vermouth.
¼ White Curaçao.
The Juice of ½ Lime.
Shake well and strain into cocktail glass.

ORIENTAL COCKTAIL.

In August, 1924, an American Engineer nearly died of fever in the Philippines, and only the extraordinary devotion of Dr. B— saved his life. As an act of gratitude the Engineer gave Dr. B— the recipe of this Cocktail.

½ Paddy Irish Whisky.
½ Italian Vermouth.
1 Dash Angostura Bitters.
Shake well and strain into cocktail glass.

PADDY COCKTAIL.

COCKTAILS

PALL MALL COCKTAIL.

1 Dash Orange Bitters.
1 Teaspoonful White Crème de Menthe.
⅓ Italian Vermouth.
⅓ French Vermouth.
⅓ Plymouth Gin.
Shake well and strain into cocktail glass.

PALMER COCKTAIL.

1 Dash Lemon Juice.
1 Dash Angostura Bitters.
1 Glass Canadian Club Whisky.
Shake well and strain into cocktail glass.

PALMETTO COCKTAIL.

2 Dashes Orange Bitters.
½ Italian Vermouth.
½ St. Croix Rum.
Shake well and strain into cocktail glass.

PANAMA COCKTAIL.

⅓ Crème de Cacao.
⅓ Sweet Cream.
⅓ Brandy.
Shake well and strain into cocktail glass.

PANSY COCKTAIL.

2 Dashes Angostura Bitters.
6 Dashes Grenadine.
1 Liqueur Glass Absinthe.
Shake well and strain into cocktail glass

COCKTAILS

2 Dashes Angostura Bitters.
1 Teaspoonful Grenadine.
1 Glass Anis del Oso.
*Shake well and strain into
   cocktail glass.*

**PANSY
BLOSSOM
COCKTAIL.**

1 Dash Orgeat Syrup.
1 Dash Grenadine.
   The White of 1 Egg.
1 Liqueur Glass French
      Vermouth.
*Shake well and strain into
   medium size glass.*

**PANTOMIME
COCKTAIL.**

1 Dash Lemon Juice.
¼ Orange Juice. ½ Gin.
¼ Apricot Brandy.
*Shake well and strain into
   cocktail glass.*

**PARADISE
COCKTAIL.**

⅓ French Vermouth.
⅓ Crème de Cassis. ⅓ Gin.
*Shake well and strain into
   cocktail glass.*

**PARISIAN
COCKTAIL.**

⅓ Sweet Cream.
⅓ Curaçao.
⅓ Jamaica Rum.
*Shake well and strain into
   cocktail glass.*

**PARISIAN
BLONDE
COCKTAIL.**

COCKTAILS

PAT'S SPECIAL COCKTAIL.
(6 people)

Put 2 Glasses of Gin, 2 of Sherry and 2 of Quinquina in the shaker ; add 2 dashes of Crème de Cassis and 2 of Abricotine. Shake well and serve with a cherry and a piece of orange peel.

PAULINE COCKTAIL.
(6 people)

3 Glasses Rum.
3 Glasses Sweetened Lemon Juice.
1 Dash Absinthe Bitters.
A little Nutmeg, grated.
Shake well and strain into cocktail glass.

PEGGY COCKTAIL.

1 Dash Absinthe.
1 Dash Dubonnet.
⅓ French Vermouth.
⅔ Dry Gin.
Shake well and strain into cocktail glass.

PEGU CLUB COCKTAIL.

1 Dash Angostura Bitters.
1 Dash Orange Bitters.
1 Teaspoonful Lime Juice
⅓ Curaçao. ⅔ Dry Gin.
Shake well and strain into cocktail glass.

The favourite cocktail of the Pegu Club, Burma, and one that has travelled, and is asked for, round the world.

PERFECT COCKTAIL.

⅓ French Vermouth.
⅓ Italian Vermouth.
⅓ Dry Gin.
Shake well and strain into cocktail glass.

COCKTAILS

1 Dash Angostura Bitters.
¼ Hercules.
¼ Applejack or Calvados.
½ Dry Gin.
Shake well and strain into
cocktail glass.

**PERSONALITY
A LA ROY
COCKTAIL.**

¼ Peach Bitters.
¼ Orange Juice.
¼ French Vermouth.
¼ Dry Gin.
Shake well and strain into
cocktail glass.

**PETER PAN
COCKTAIL.**

The Juice of ¼ Orange.
¼ French Vermouth.
¼ Italian Vermouth.
½ Plymouth Gin.
2 Dashes Maraschino.
Shake well and strain into
cocktail glass.

**PETO
COCKTAIL.**

1 Hooker Applejack.
1 Hooker Port.
The Juice of 1 Orange.
Place in tumbler and fill up with
ginger ale.

**PHILADELPHIA
SCOTCHMAN
COCKTAIL.**

2½ Glasses of Sherry.
1 Glass Rum.
1½ Glasses Quinquina.
1½ Glasses Orange Juice.
Give one grind of the peppermill
over this. Shake : serve !

**PHILOMEL
COCKTAIL.
(6 people)***

* After which they all sing like nightingales.
Whence the name.

121

COCKTAILS

PHOEBE SNOW COCKTAIL.
1 Dash Absinthe.
½ Brandy
½ Dubonnet.
Shake well and strain into cocktail glass.

PICCAD COCKTAIL.
3 Dashes Angostura Bitters.
½ Caperitif.
½ Dry Gin.
Shake well with two or three pieces of lemon rind and strain.

PICCADILLY COCKTAIL.
1 Dash Absinthe.
1 Dash Grenadine.
⅓ French Vermouth.
⅔ Dry Gin.
Shake well and strain into cocktail glass.

Mr. George Washington Bronx writing to the "Times" explaining how he invented the cocktails bearing his name.

½ Italian Vermouth. ½ Amer Picon. *Shake well and strain into cocktail glass.*	PICON COCKTAIL.
1 Liqueur Glass Amer Picon. ½ Liqueur Glass Grenadine. *Use medium size glass and fill with soda water.*	PICON AND GRENADINE COCKTAIL.
First take a glass of fresh pineapple juice. Soak the fruit from which this juice has been extracted for two hours in 2 glasses of Dry White Wine. Mix these together, adding as well the juice of a quarter of a lemon; and pour the whole into the shaker with 3 glasses of Sherry. Stand the shaker in ice, but do not put any ice into the mixture. Shake, strain and serve with a small piece of pineapple in the glass. This is a very mild cocktail.	PINEAPPLE COCKTAIL. (6 people)
The Juice of ¼ Lemon. ½ Sloe Gin. ½ Crème Yvette. *Shake well and strain into cocktail glass.*	PING-PONG COCKTAIL.

PING-PONG SPECIAL COCKTAIL. (6 people)

Carefully shake together 3 glasses of Sloe Gin and 3 glasses of Italian Vermouth, with half a dessertspoonful of Angostura Bitters and a dessertspoonful of sugar syrup or Curaçao. Serve with a cherry and a piece of lemon rind.

PINK BABY COCKTAIL.

½ Gin. ¼ Grenadine.
¼ Sirop-de-Citron.
The White of 1 Egg.
Shake well and strain into medium size glass.

PINK GIN COCKTAIL.

1 Dash Angostura Bitters.
1 Glass Gin.
Shake well and strain into cocktail glass.

PINK LADY COCKTAIL.

The White of 1 Egg.
1 Tablespoonful Grenadine.
1 Glass Plymouth Gin.
Shake well and strain into medium size glass.

PINK PEARL COCKTAIL. (6 people)

Take 1½ glasses of grapefruit juice, a dessertspoonful of lemon juice, ½ a dessertspoonful of grenadine syrup, and the white of one egg. Add plenty of crushed ice and shake thoroughly.

COCKTAILS

PINK ROSE COCKTAIL.

The White of 1 Egg.
1 Teaspoonful Grenadine.
1 Teaspoonful Lemon Juice.
1 Teaspoonful Sweet Cream.
⅔ Glass Dry Gin.
Shake well and strain into cocktail glass.

PINKY COCKTAIL.

The White of 1 Egg.
½ Grenadine.
½ Dry Gin.
Shake well and strain into cocktail glass.

PLAIN SHERRY COCKTAIL.
(6 people)

Pour into the shaker 6 glasses of Sherry, a few drops of Absinthe Bitters, and a few drops of Maraschino. Shake very thoroughly and serve.

PLAIN VERMOUTH COCKTAIL.
(6 people)

5½ Glasses French Vermouth.
1 Teaspoonful Absinthe Bitters.
1 Teaspoonful Maraschino.
Shake very thoroughly and serve with a cherry.

PLANTER'S COCKTAIL.
(No. 1.)

1 Dash Lemon Juice
½ Orange Juice.
½ Rum.
Shake well and strain into cocktail glass.

COCKTAILS

PLANTER'S
COCKTAIL.
(No. 2.)

¼ Lemon Juice.
¼ Syrup.
½ Jamaica Rum.
*Shake well and strain into
cocktail glass.*

PLANTER'S COCKTAIL.
This drink is greatly favoured by Planters, particularly in Jamaica, where Rum is good and cheap.

PLAZA
COCKTAIL.

⅓ Italian Vermouth.
⅓ French Vermouth.
⅓ Dry Gin.
1 Slice of Pineapple.
*Shake well and strain into
cocktail glass.*

POKER
COCKTAIL.

½ Italian Vermouth.
½ Bacardi Rum.
*Shake well and strain into
cocktail glass.*

POLO
COCKTAIL.
(No. 1.)

The Juice of ¼ Lemon or
½ Lime.
⅓ Italian Vermouth.
⅓ French Vermouth.
⅓ Dry Gin.
*Shake well and strain into
cocktail glass.*

POLO
COCKTAIL.
(No. 2.)

⅙ Grape Fruit Juice.
⅙ Orange Juice.
⅔ Plymouth Gin.
*Shake well and strain into
cocktail glass.*

COCKTAILS

⅓ Bacardi Rum.
1 Dash Apricot Brandy.
⅓ Swedish Punch.
⅓ Dry Gin.
*Shake well and strain into
cocktail glass.*

POOH-BAH
COCKTAIL.

½ Blackberry Brandy.
¼ Port Wine.
¼ Brandy.
*Shake well and strain into
cocktail glass.*

POOP DECK
COCKTAIL.

⅓ Crème de Cacao.
⅔ Dry Gin.
*Shake well and strain into
cocktail glass.*

POPPY
COCKTAIL.

1 Dash Brandy.
1 Glass Port Wine.
*Stir slightly in ice and strain.
Squeeze orange peel on top.*

PORT WINE
COCKTAIL.
(No. 1.)

1 Dash Angostura Bitters.
1 Dash Orange Bitters.
2 Dashes Curaçao.
1 Glass Port Wine.
*Stir well and strain into Port
Wine glass.*

PORT WINE
COCKTAIL.
(No. 2.)

2 Dashes Vinegar.
1 Teaspoonful Worcester-
shire Sauce.
1 Egg.
2 Dashes Tabasco Sauce.
A little Pepper and Salt.
Do not break the Egg.

PRAIRIE
HEN
COCKTAIL.

COCKTAILS

PRAIRIE OYSTER COCKTAIL.	2 Dashes Vinegar. The Yolk of 1 Egg. 1 Teaspoonful Worcestershire Sauce. 1 Teaspoonful Tomato Catsup. 1 Dash of Pepper on Top. *Do not break the Yolk of Egg.*
PRESIDENT COCKTAIL.	2 Dashes Grenadine. The Juice of ¼ Orange. 1 Glass Bacardi Rum. *Shake well and strain into cocktail glass.*
PRESTO COCKTAIL.	1 Dash Absinthe. ⅙ Orange Juice. ⅙ Italian Vermouth. ⅔ Brandy. *Shake well and strain into cocktail glass.*
PRINCESS COCKTAIL.	¾ Apricot Brandy. ¼ Sweet Cream. *Use liqueur glass and pour Cream carefully so that it does not mix.*

By the Way.—Malicious tongues assert stance produced by Bar-leaning: London, Paris, Havana and New York.

COCKTAILS

⅓ Crème de Cacao.
⅓ Sweet Cream.
⅓ Dry Gin.
*Shake well and strain into
cocktail glass.*

**PRINCESS
MARY
COCKTAIL.**

¼ French Vermouth.
¼ Dubonnet.
½ Calvados.
*Shake well and strain into
cocktail glass.*

**PRINCESS
MARY'S PRIDE
COCKTAIL.**

Created by Harry Craddock on February 28,
1922, to mark the wedding celebrations of H.R.H.
Princess Mary.

1 Dash Lemon Juice.
¼ Apricot Brandy.
¼ Calvados or Apple Brandy.
½ Dry Gin.
*Shake well and strain into
cocktail glass.*

**PRINCE'S
SMILE
COCKTAIL.**

2 Dashes Orange Bitters.
⅓ Port Wine.
⅔ Tom Gin.
*Stir well and strain into cock-
tail glass. Squeeze lemon peel
on top.*

**PRINCETON
COCKTAIL.**

½ Plymouth Gin.
½ Kina Lillet.
2 Dashes Orange Juice.
1 Dash Apricot Brandy.
*Shake well and strain into cock-
tail glass. Squeeze lemon peel
on top.*

**PROHIBITION
COCKTAIL.**

COCKTAILS

PRUNEAUX COCKTAIL. (6 people)	2 Glasses of Gin, 2 of Sherry, 1 of Syrup of Prunes and 1 of strained Orange Juice. Shake thoroughly in cracked ice, and serve.
QUAKER'S COCKTAIL.	⅓ Brandy. ⅓ Rum. ⅙ Lemon Juice. ⅙ Raspberry Syrup. *Shake well and strain into cocktail glass.*
QUARTER DECK COCKTAIL.	1 Teaspoonful of Lime Juice. ⅓ Sherry. ⅔ Rum. *Shake well and strain into cocktail glass.*
QUEEN'S COCKTAIL.	½ Slice of Crushed Pineapple. ¼ French Vermouth. ¼ Italian Vermouth. ½ Gin. *Shake well and strain into cocktail glass.*
QUEEN ELIZABETH COCKTAIL.	1 Dash Absinthe. ¼ Lemon Juice. ¼ Cointreau. ½ Dry Gin. *Shake well and strain into cocktail glass.*
QUEEN ELIZABETH COCKTAIL.	1 Dash Curaçao. ½ Italian Vermouth. ½ Brandy. *Stir well and strain into cocktail glass. Add 1 cherry.*

COCKTAILS

⅓ Kummel. ⅔ Brandy.
*Stir well and strain into
cocktail glass.*

**QUELLE VIE
COCKTAIL.**

Brandy gives you courage and Kummel makes you cautious, thus giving you a perfect mixture of bravery and caution, with the bravery predominating.

2 Dashes Orange Bitters.
¼ French Vermouth.
¼ Italian Vermouth.
½ Dry Gin.
*Shake well and strain into cocktail glass. Squeeze orange peel
on top.*

**R.A.C.
SPECIAL
COCKTAIL.**

1 Dash Orange Bitters.
⅓ French Vermouth.
⅔ Plymouth Gin.
*Shake well and strain into
cocktail glass.*

**RACQUET
CLUB
COCKTAIL.**

⅐ Crème de Cacao.
⅐ Crème de Violette.
⅐ Yellow Chartreuse.
⅐ Maraschino.
⅐ Bénédictine.
⅐ Green Chartreuse.
⅐ Brandy.
*Use liqueur glass and pour ingredients carefully so that they do not
mix.*

**RAINBOW
COCKTAIL.**

¼ Hercules.
¼ French Vermouth.
½ Dry Gin.
*Shake well and strain into cocktail glass. Squeeze orange peel
on top.*

**RAMON
NEWTON
COCKTAIL.**

COCKTAILS

**RASPBERRY COCKTAIL.
(6 people)**

Slightly bruise a cupful of fresh raspberries and add 2 glasses of Gin. Soak for two hours and strain. Complete the mixture by adding a liqueur glass of Kirsch and 2 glasses of any White Wine which is not too sweet, such as Moselle, Graves or Chablis. Ice. Shake. Put a raspberry in each glass, and serve.

This is a very refreshing summer cocktail.

**RATTLE-SNAKE COCKTAIL.*
(6 people)**

4 Glasses Rye Whisky.
The Whites of 2 Eggs.
1 Glass Sweetened Lemon Juice.
A Few Dashes Absinthe.
Shake very thoroughly and serve by straining it through a fine sieve.

* So called because it will either cure Rattlesnake bite, or kill Rattlesnakes, or make you see them.

RAY LONG COCKTAIL.

1 Dash Angostura Bitters.
4 Dashes Absinthe.
⅓ Glass Italian Vermouth.
⅔ Glass Brandy.
Shake well and strain into cocktail glass.

COCKTAILS

RAYMOND HITCH COCKTAIL.

The Juice of ½ Orange.
1 Dash Orange Bitters.
1 Slice Pineapple.
1 Glass Italian Vermouth.
Shake well and strain into cocktail glass.

REFORM COCKTAIL.

1 Dash Orange Bitters.
⅓ French Vermouth.
⅔ Sherry.
Stir well and strain into cocktail glass. Add a cherry.

RESOLUTE COCKTAIL.

¼ Lemon Juice.
¼ Apricot Brandy.
½ Dry Gin.
Shake well and strain into cocktail glass.

RE-VIGORATOR COCKTAIL.

½ Gin. ¼ Kola Tonic.
¼ Sirop-de-Citron.
Shake well and strain into cocktail glass.

COCKTAIL TIME IN LOUISIANA 1843

COCKTAILS

RICHMOND COCKTAIL.

⅓ Kina Lillet.
⅔ Plymouth Gin.
Shake well and strain into cocktail glass. Squeeze lemon peel on top.

⅛ Lemon Juice.
⅛ Orange Juice.
¼ Grenadine.
½ Jamaica Rum.
Shake well and strain into cocktail glass.

ROBSON COCKTAIL.

1 Dash Angostura Bitters.
½ Italian Vermouth.
½ Scotch Whisky.
Shake well and strain into cocktail glass.
Particularly for Saint Andrew's Day, to open the evening for the usual enormous annual gathering of the Clans at the Savoy.

ROB ROY COCKTAIL.

½ Sherry. ½ Dry Gin.
Stir well and strain into cocktail glass. Add a cherry.

ROC-A-COE COCKTAIL.

1 Glass Rye Whisky, or Canadian Club.
Dissolve 1 Piece of Rock Candy in it.
The Juice of 1 Lemon can be added if desired.

ROCK AND RYE COCKTAIL.

COCKTAILS

ROLLS ROYCE COCKTAIL.

1 Dash Bénédictine.
¼ French Vermouth.
¼ Italian Vermouth.
½ Dry Gin.
Shake well and strain into cocktail glass.

ROSE COCKTAIL. (ENGLISH)

1 Dash Lemon Juice.
4 Dashes Grenadine.
¼ Apricot Brandy.
¼ French Vermouth.
½ Dry Gin.
Shake well and strain into cocktail glass. Frost edge of cocktail glass with castor sugar.

ROSE COCKTAIL. (FRENCH STYLE No. 1.)

¼ Cherry Brandy.
¼ French Vermouth.
½ Dry Gin.
Stir well and strain into cocktail glass.

ROSE COCKTAIL. (FRENCH STYLE No. 2.)

¼ Cherry Brandy.
¼ Kirsch.
½ Dry Gin.
Stir well and strain into cocktail glass.

ROSE COCKTAIL. (FRENCH STYLE No. 3.)

1 Teaspoonful Grenadine.
½ French Vermouth.
½ Kirsch.
Shake well and strain into cocktail glass.

COCKTAILS

2 Dashes Grenadine.
1/3 French Vermouth.
2/3 Dry Gin.
Shake well and strain into cocktail glass. Squeeze lemon peel on top.

ROSELYN COCKTAIL.

1/3 Italian Vermouth.
2/3 Dry Gin.
Shake well and strain into cocktail glass. Squeeze orange peel on top.

ROSINGTON COCKTAIL.

1/4 Swedish Punch.
1/4 Bacardi Rum.
1/2 Calvados.
Shake well and strain into cocktail glass.

ROULETTE COCKTAIL.

The Juice of 1/2 Lemon.
1/2 Tablespoonful Powdered Sugar.
1 Egg.
1 Glass Dry Gin.
Shake well and strain into medium size glass.

ROYAL COCKTAIL. (No. 1.)

1/3 French Vermouth.
1/3 Dry Gin.
1/3 Cherry Brandy.
Stir well and strain into cocktail glass.

ROYAL COCKTAIL. (No. 2.)

COCKTAILS

ROYAL COCKTAIL.
(No: 3)

⅓ Gin.
⅓ French Vermouth.
⅓ Cherry Brandy.
1 Dash Maraschino.
Shake well and strain into·cocktail glass, with cherry.

ROYAL CLOVER CLUB COCKTAIL.

The Juice of ½ Lemon.
1 Tablespoonful Grenadine.
The Yolk of 1 Egg.
1 Glass Gin.
Shake well and strain into medium size glass.

ROYAL SMILE COCKTAIL.

The Juice of ¼ Lemon.
¼ Grenadine.
½ Applejack or Calvados.
¼ Dry Gin.
Shake well and strain into cocktail glass.

ROY HOWARD COCKTAIL.

½ Glass Kina Lillet.
¼ Glass Brandy.
¼ Glass Orange Juice.
2 Dashes Grenadine.
Shake well and strain into cocktail glass.

RUSSELL HOUSE COCKTAIL.

2 Dashes Orange Bitters.
2 Dashes Syrup.
3 Dashes Blackberry Brandy.
1 Glass Canadian Club Whisky.
Shake well and strain into cocktail glass.

COCKTAILS

⅓ Crème de Cacao.
⅓ Dry Gin.
⅓ Vodka.
Shake well, strain into cocktail glass, and tossitoff quickski.

RUSSIAN COCKTAIL.

1 Dash Angostura Bitters.
4 Dashes Syrup.
1 Glass Rye or Canadian Club Whisky.
Stir well and strain into cocktail glass. Add 1 cherry.

RYE WHISKY COCKTAIL.

The Juice of ½ Lemon and ¼ Grapefruit.
The White of 1 Egg.
1 Liqueur Glass Green Chartreuse.
Shake well and strain into cocktail glass.

ST. GERMAIN COCKTAIL.

An attempt to translate: "This hooch is the Cat's Pyjamas," from North American into fluent Russian.

Tremendous enthusiasm of an American Citizen, sighting the Statue of Liberty for the first time, after a world tour that started from San Francisco.

ST. MARK COCKTAIL.	1/6 Groseille. 1/3 Burrough's Beefeater Gin. 1/6 Cherry Brandy. 1/3 French Vermouth. *Shake well and strain into cocktail glass.*
SALOMÉ COCKTAIL.	1/3 French Vermouth. 1/3 Dry Gin. 1/3 Dubonnet. *Shake well and strain into cocktail glass.*
SANCTUARY COCKTAIL.*	1/4 Cointreau. 1/4 Amer Picon. 1/2 Dubonnet. *Shake well and strain into cocktail glass.*

* So-called because the Savoy, together with The Clink, Deadman's Place, Fulwood's Rents, The Mint, Mitre Court, Baldwin's Gardens and Stepney were the last places in London where the privilege of " Sanctuary " existed. Unfortunately this privilege was abolished by " The Escape from Prison Act " in 1697. But even to-day no Ladies are allowed in the Savoy's inner American Cocktail Bar.

COCKTAILS

1 Teaspoonful Green Chartreuse.
½ Italian Vermouth.
½ Dry Gin.
Shake well and strain into cocktail glass.

SAND-MARTIN COCKTAIL.

2 Dashes Grenadine.
2 Dashes Lemon Juice.
1 Glass Bacardi Rum.
Shake well and strain into cocktail glass.

SANTIAGO COCKTAIL.

2 Dashes Maraschino.
2 Dashes Angostura Bitters.
¼ Slice Pineapple.
1 Glass Brandy.
Shake well and strain, adding a little soda water.

SARATOGA COCKTAIL.

1 Dash Apricot Brandy.
1 Dash Absinthe.
½ Calvados.   ½ Brandy.
Stir well and squeeze orange peel on top.

SAUCY SUE COCKTAIL.

COCKTAILS

SATAN'S WHISKERS COCKTAIL. (Straight) Of Italian Vermouth, French Vermouth, Gin and Orange Juice, two parts each; of Grand Marnier one part; Orange Bitters, a dash.
Shake well and strain into cocktail glass.

SATAN'S WHISKERS COCKTAIL. (Curled) For the Grand Marnier in the foregoing Cocktail, substitute the same quantity of Orange Curaçao.
Shake well and strain into cocktail glass.

SAVOY HOTEL COCKTAIL.
$1/3$ Crème de Cacao. $1/3$ Bénédictine. $1/3$ Brandy. *Use liqueur glass and pour ingredients carefully, so that they do not mix.*

SAVOY HOTEL SPECIAL COCKTAIL.* (No. 1.)
1 Dash Absinthe.
2 Dashes Grenadine.
$1/3$ French Vermouth.
$2/3$ Dry Gin.
Shake well and strain into cocktail glass. Squeeze lemon peel on top.

* Peter, ninth Earl of Savoy, brought to England, as his wards, eighty-three of the most wealthy and beautiful girls in France. He then married them to the most powerful nobles in England. That is why he wore armour

COCKTAILS

2 Dashes Dubonnet.
⅓ French Vermouth.
⅔ Plymouth Gin.
Shake well and strain into cocktail glass. Squeeze orange peel on top.

SAVOY HOTEL SPECIAL COCKTAIL. (No. 2.)

½ Sloe Gin.
½ Applejack or Calvados.
Shake well and strain into cocktail glass.

SAVOY TANGO COCKTAIL.

This cocktail is a very great favourite at the Savoy Hotel, London, where it was invented.

1 Lump of Sugar.
1 Dash Angostura or Peychana Bitters.
1 Glass Rye or Canadian Club Whisky.
Stir well and strain into another glass that has been cooled, add 1 dash Absinthe and squeeze lemon peel on top.

SAZERAC COCKTAIL.

1 Dash Orange Bitters.
⅓ Canadian Club Whisky.
⅓ French Vermouth.
⅙ Lemon Juice.
⅙ Grenadine.
Shake well and strain into cocktail glass.

SCOFF-LAW COCKTAIL.

COCKTAILS

SELF-STARTER COCKTAIL.
- 1/8 Apricot Brandy.
- 3/8 Kina Lillet.
- 1/2 Dry Gin.
- 2 Dashes Absinthe.

Shake well and strain into cocktail glass.

SENSATION COCKTAIL.
- 3 Dashes Maraschino.
- 3 Sprigs Fresh Mint.
- 1/4 Lemon Juice.
- 3/4 Dry Gin.

Shake well and strain into cocktail glass.

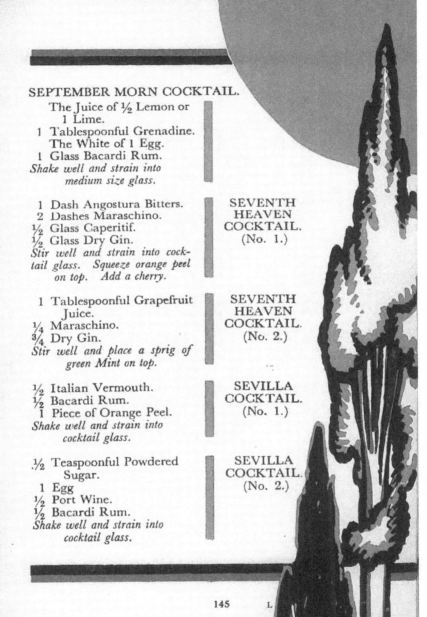

SEPTEMBER MORN COCKTAIL.
The Juice of ½ Lemon or 1 Lime.
1 Tablespoonful Grenadine.
The White of 1 Egg.
1 Glass Bacardi Rum.
Shake well and strain into medium size glass.

1 Dash Angostura Bitters.
2 Dashes Maraschino.
½ Glass Caperitif.
½ Glass Dry Gin.
Stir well and strain into cocktail glass. Squeeze orange peel on top. Add a cherry.

SEVENTH HEAVEN COCKTAIL. (No. 1.)

1 Tablespoonful Grapefruit Juice.
¼ Maraschino.
¾ Dry Gin.
Stir well and place a sprig of green Mint on top.

SEVENTH HEAVEN COCKTAIL. (No. 2.)

½ Italian Vermouth.
½ Bacardi Rum.
1 Piece of Orange Peel.
Shake well and strain into cocktail glass.

SEVILLA COCKTAIL. (No. 1.)

½ Teaspoonful Powdered Sugar.
1 Egg
½ Port Wine.
½ Bacardi Rum.
Shake well and strain into cocktail glass.

SEVILLA COCKTAIL. (No. 2.)

COCKTAILS

" S.G." COCKTAIL.

1 Teaspoonful Grenadine.
⅓ Canadian Club Whisky.
⅓ Lemon Juice.
⅓ Orange Juice.
Shake well and strain into cocktail glass.

This Cocktail is very popular in the Officers' Mess of the Scots Guards, hence its name.

SHAMROCK COCKTAIL.

3 Dashes Green Crème de Menthe.
3 Dashes Green Chartreuse.
½ French Vermouth.
½ Irish Whisky.
Shake well and strain into cocktail glass.

SHANGHAI COCKTAIL.

2 Dashes Grenadine.
⅜ Lemon Juice.
⅛ Anisette.
½ Jamaica Rum.
Shake well and strain into cocktail glass.

SHARKY PUNCH COCKTAIL.

1 Teaspoonful Syrup
¼ Canadian Club Whisky.
¾ Calvados or Apple Brandy.
Shake well and strain into medium size glass and fill with soda water.

SHERRY COCKTAIL.

4 Dashes Orange Bitters.
4 Dashes French Vermouth.
1 Glass Sherry.
Stir well and strain into cocktail glass.

COCKTAILS

Place an Egg in Large Port Wine Glass, being careful not to break the yolk.
Fill glass with Sherry.

SHERRY AND EGG COCKTAIL.

1 Glass Brandy.
1 Glass French Vermouth.
3 Glasses Sherry.
⅔ Glass Cointreau.
⅓ Glass Lemon Juice.
1 Small Piece Cinnamon.
Shake well and strain into cocktail glass.

SHERRY TWIST COCKTAIL.
(No. 1)
(6 people)

Take the juice of 1 Orange, 2 glasses of Whisky, 2½ glasses of Sherry and ½ glass of Cointreau. Add two cloves, squeeze in the juice of ¼ lemon, and add half a turn of the pepper-mill. Fill the shaker with cracked ice.
Shake and serve.

SHERRY TWIST COCKTAIL.
(No. 2)
(6 people)

4 Glasses Sherry.
1 Glass Whisky.
1 Glass Rum.
1 Glass Prune Syrup.
1 Dash Orange Bitters.
   A little Sugar if desired.
Shake well and strain into cocktail glass.

SHIP COCKTAIL.
(6 people)

¼ Lemon Juice.
¼ Cointreau.   ½ Brandy.
Shake well and strain into cocktail glass.

SIDECAR COCKTAIL.

COCKTAILS

SILVER COCKTAIL.

2 Dashes Maraschino.
2 Dashes Orange Bitters.
½ French Vermouth.
½ Dry Gin.
Shake well and strain into
cocktail glass.

SILVER BULLET COCKTAIL.

½ Gin.
¼ Lemon Juice.
¼ Kummel.
Shake well and strain into
cocktail glass.

SILVER KING COCKTAIL.

The Juice of ¼ Lemon.
1 Teaspoonful Sugar.
2 Dashes Orange Bitters.
The White of 1 Egg.
1 Glass Plymouth Gin.
Shake well and strain into
cocktail glass.

SILVER STALLION COCKTAIL.

½ Vanilla Ice Cream.
½ Gin.
Fill with Silver Fizz, *q.v. p. 200.*

SILVER STREAK COCKTAIL.

½ Kummel.
½ Dry Gin.
Shake well and strain into
cocktail glass.

SIR WALTER COCKTAIL.
(commonly known as the "Swalter.")

1 Teaspoonful Grenadine.
1 Teaspoonful Curaçao.
1 Teaspoonful Lemon Juice.
⅓ Brandy.
⅓ Rum.
Shake well and strain into
cocktail glass.

COCKTAILS

1 Glass Brandy.
1 Piece of Orange Peel.
4 Leaves of Fresh Mint.
Fill long tumbler with Ginger Ale.

SLEEPY HEAD COCKTAIL.

¼ French Vermouth.
¼ Italian Vermouth.
½ Sloe Gin.
Stir well and strain into cocktail glass.

SLOE GIN COCKTAIL.

1 Dash Angostura Bitters.
1 Dash Orange Bitters.
1 Glass Sloe Gin.
Shake well and strain into cocktail glass.

SLOEBERRY COCKTAIL.

1 Dash Angostura Bitters.
1 Dash Orange Juice.
¼ Italian Vermouth.
¼ French Vermouth.
½ Dry Gin.
Shake well and strain into cocktail glass.

SMILER COCKTAIL.

COCKTAILS

SNICKER COCKTAIL.

The White of 1 Egg.
2 Dashes Maraschino.
1 Teaspoonful Syrup.
1 Dash Orange Bitters.
⅓ French Vermouth.
⅔ Dry Gin.
Shake well and strain into medium size glass.

SNOWBALL COCKTAIL.

⅙ Crème de Violette.
⅙ White Crème de Menthe.
⅙ Anisette.
⅙ Sweet Cream.
⅓ Dry Gin.
Shake well and strain into cocktail glass.
This is woman's work.

SNYDER COCKTAIL.

⅓ French Vermouth.
⅔ Dry Gin.
3 Dashes Curaçao.
Shake well and strain into cocktail glass. Twist orange peel on top.

SODA COCKTAIL.

1 Lump of Sugar.
4 Dashes Angostura Bitters.
1 Lump of Ice.
Use long tumbler and fill with a bottle of lemon soda, or lemonade.

SOME MOTH COCKTAIL.

1 Dash Absinthe.
⅓ French Vermouth.
⅔ Plymouth Gin.
Shake well and strain into cocktail glass. Add 1 pearl onion.

SONORA COCKTAIL.

1 Dash Lemon Juice.
2 Dashes Apricot Brandy.
½ Applejack or Calvados.
½ Bacardi Rum.
Shake well and strain into cocktail glass.

SONZA'S WILSON COCKTAIL.

½ Gin. ½ Cherry Brandy.
4 Dashes Lemon Juice or Lime Juice.
4 Dashes Grenadine.
Shake well and strain into cocktail glass.

SO-SO COCKTAIL.

1/6 Grenadine.
1/6 Calvados.
⅓ Italian Vermouth.
⅓ Dry Gin.
Shake well and strain into cocktail glass.

SOUL KISS COCKTAIL. (No. 1.)

1/6 Orange Juice.
1/6 Dubonnet.
⅓ French Vermouth.
⅓ Italian Vermouth.
Shake well and strain into cocktail glass.

SOUL KISS COCKTAIL. (No. 2.)

1/6 Orange Juice.
1/6 Dubonnet.
⅓ French Vermouth.
⅓ Canadian Club Whisky.
1 Slice of Orange.
Shake well and strain into cocktail glass.

SOUTHERN GIN COCKTAIL.	2 Dashes Curaçao. 2 Dashes Orange Bitters. 1 Glass Dry Gin. *Shake well and strain into cocktail glass.*
SOUTH SIDE COCKTAIL.	The Juice of ½ Lemon. ½ Tablespoonful of Powdered Sugar. 2 Sprigs Fresh Mint. 1 Glass Dry Gin. *Shake well and strain into medium size glass. Add dash of siphon soda water.*
SOYER-AU-CHAMPAGNE COCKTAIL.	1 Liqueur Glass Ice Cream. 2 Dashes Maraschino. 2 Dashes Curaçao. 2 Dashes Brandy. *Stir well together in medium size glass and fill with Champagne. Add slice of pineapple or orange, 1 cherry or strawberry.*
SPANISH TOWN COCKTAIL. (6 people)	5 Glasses Rum. 1 Dessertspoonful Curaçao. *Pour into shaker, add a large quantity of ice, and shake thoroughly. Grate a little nutmeg over each glass and serve.*

COCKTAILS

1 Dash Absinthe.
½ Applejack (known in America as "Jersey Lightning").
½ Brandy.
Serve very cold.

SPECIAL ROUGH COCKTAIL.

1 Dash Angostura Bitters.
1 Dash Orange Juice.
⅓ Apricot Brandy.
⅔ Dry Gin.
Shake well and strain into cocktail glass Add a cherry and squeeze orange peel on top.

SPENCER COCKTAIL.

Very mellifluous: has a fine and rapid action: for morning work.

½ French Vermouth.
½ Caperitif.
Stir well and strain into cocktail glass.

SPION KOP COCKTAIL.

3 Glasses Gin.
1 Glass Quinquina.
1 Glass Bénédictine.
Before shaking add a dash of bitters and serve with an olive.

**SPRING COCKTAIL.
(6 people)**

¼ Lemon Juice.
¼ Green Chartreuse.
½ Plymouth Gin.
Shake well and strain into cocktail glass.

SPRING FEELING COCKTAIL.

COCKTAILS

STANLEY COCKTAIL.

$\frac{1}{6}$ Lemon Juice.
$\frac{1}{6}$ Grenadine.
$\frac{1}{3}$ Gin. $\frac{1}{3}$ Rum.
*Shake well and strain into
cocktail glass.*

STAR COCKTAIL. (No. 1.)

1 Teaspoonful Grape Fruit Juice.
1 Dash Italian Vermouth.
1 Dash French Vermouth.
$\frac{1}{2}$ Calvados or Apple Brandy.
$\frac{1}{2}$ Dry Gin.
*Shake well and strain into
cocktail glass.*

STAR COCKTAIL. (No. 2.)

$\frac{1}{2}$ Italian Vermouth.
$\frac{1}{2}$ Applejack or Calvados.
*Shake well and strain into
cocktail glass.*

STARS AND STRIPES.

$\frac{1}{3}$ Crème de Cassis.
$\frac{1}{3}$ Maraschino.
$\frac{1}{3}$ Green Chartreuse.
*Use liqueur glass and pour care-
fully so that ingredients do not mix.*

STINGER COCKTAIL.

$\frac{1}{4}$ White Crème de Menthe.
$\frac{3}{4}$ Brandy.
*Shake well and strain into
cocktail glass.*

STOMACH REVIVER COCKTAIL.

5 Dashes Angostura Bitters.
$\frac{1}{6}$ Fernet Branca.
$\frac{2}{3}$ Brandy. $\frac{2}{3}$ Kummel.
*Shake well and strain into
cocktail glass.*

COCKTAILS

1 Lump of Ice.
2 Dashes Angostura Bitters.
1 Glass Scotch Whisky.
*Use long tumbler and fill with
    soda water.*

**STONE
FENCE.**

⅓ Dry Gin.
⅔ Dry Sherry.
*Shake well and strain into
    cocktail glass.*

**STRAIGHT
LAW
COCKTAIL.**

Pass 1 lb. of strawberries
through a hair-sieve, and
pour the juice into the shaker,
together with the juice of an
orange and a dash of Whisky.
Add a few pieces of ice.
    Shake carefully and serve.

**STRAWBERRY
COCKTAIL
(6 people)**

¼ Lemon or Lime Juice.
¼ Swedish Punch.
½ Gin.
*Shake well and strain into
    cocktail glass.*

**STRIKE'S
OFF
COCKTAIL.**

Created by Harry Craddock on May 12, 1926, to
mark the end of the General Strike.

The White of 1 Egg.
4 Dashes Anisette.
1 Liqueur Glass Absinthe.
    Syrup or Sugar can be
        used   instead   of
        Anisette.
*Shake well and strain into
    medium size glass.*

**SUISSE
COCKTAIL.**

COCKTAILS

SUMMER TIME COCKTAIL.

¾ Gin.
¼ Sirop-de-Citron.
Shake well and strain into medium size glass; fill up with soda water.

SUNRISE.

¼ Grenadine.
¼ Crème de Violette.
¼ Yellow Chartreuse.
¼ Cointreau.
Use liqueur glass and pour ingredients in carefully so that they do not mix.

SUNSET COCKTAIL.
(6 people)

Place in a large glass the thinly-cut rind of an orange, or of a tangerine if an orange cannot be obtained. Add a teaspoonful of peach preserve, a large apricot and its crushed kernel. Pour upon the whole a full glass of Brandy and a small spoonful of Kirsch. Let this soak for two hours. Then transfer the mixture into the shaker and add half a glass of White Wine, a glass and half of Gin, and a glass of French Vermouth. Add plenty of ice. *Shake and serve.*

The next thing you know about is *Sunrise.*

COCKTAILS

SUNSHINE COCKTAIL. (No. 1.)

1 Dash Angostura Bitters.
⅓ Italian Vermouth.
⅔ Dry Gin.
1 Lump of Ice.
Stir well and strain into medium size glass. Squeeze orange peel on top.

SUNSHINE COCKTAIL. (No. 2.)

The Juice of ¼ Lemon.
2 Dashes Crème de Cassis.
½ French Vermouth.
½ Bacardi Rum.
Shake well and strain into cocktail glass.

Mr. ERIC SUTTON'S GIN BLIND COCKTAIL.*

6 Parts Gin.
3 Parts Curaçao.
2 Parts Brandy.
1 Dash Orange Bitters.

* Invented by THE Mr. Sutton. Chelsea Papers please copy. This is a very troublesome form of refreshment.

SWAZI FREEZE COCKTAIL.

1 Dash Peach Brandy.
⅓ Canadian Club Whisky.
⅔ Caperitif.
Stir well and strain into cocktail glass.

COCKTAILS

SWEET PATOTIE COCKTAIL.

¼ Orange Juice.
¼ Cointreau.
½ Dry Gin.
Shake well and strain into cocktail glass.

SWIZZLES COCKTAIL.

The Juice of 1 Lime.
1 Dash Angostura Bitters.
1 Glass of Gin.
1 Teaspoonful of Sugar.
Stir with swizzle stick until it foams.

TANGLEFOOT COCKTAIL.

⅙ Orange Juice.
⅙ Lemon Juice.
⅓ Bacardi Rum.
⅓ Swedish Punch.
Shake well and strain into cocktail glass.

TANGO COCKTAIL.

2 Dashes Curaçao.
The Juice of ¼ Orange.
¼ French Vermouth.
¼ Italian Vermouth.
½ Dry Gin.
Shake well and strain into cocktail glass.

TANTALUS COCKTAIL.

⅓ Lemon Juice.
⅓ Brandy.
⅓ Forbidden Fruit Liqueur.
Shake well and strain into cocktail glass.

COCKTAILS

1 Piece Orange Peel.
1 Piece Lemon Peel.
2 Dashes Dubonnet.
2 Dashes Absinthe.
2 Dashes Curaçao.
1 Glass Canadian Club
  Whisky.
*Shake well and strain into
  cocktail glass.*

**TEMPTATION
COCKTAIL.**

½ Port Wine.
½ Apricot Brandy.
*Shake well and strain into
  cocktail glass.*

**TEMPTER
COCKTAIL.**

⅔ Burrough's Plymouth Gin.
⅓ French Vermouth.
4 Dashes of Absinthe.
*Shake well and strain into old-
  fashioned whisky glass.*

**THIRD
DEGREE
COCKTAIL.**

1 Dash White Mint.
1 Dash Curaçao.
1 Glass French Vermouth.
*Shake well and strain into
  cocktail glass.*

**THIRD RAIL
COCKTAIL.
(No. 1.)**

1 Dash Absinthe.
⅓ Bacardi Rum.
⅓ Calvados or Apple Brandy.
⅓ Brandy.
*Shake well and strain into
  cocktail glass.*

**THIRD RAIL
COCKTAIL.
(No. 2.)**

Simply splendid   Better than 11,000 volts.

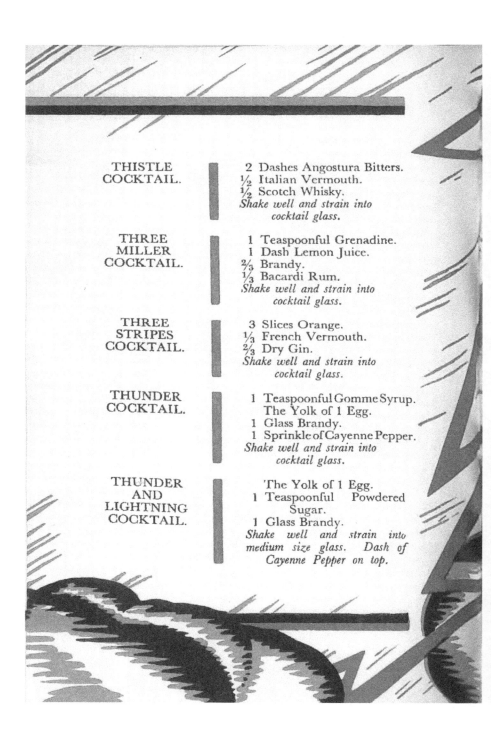

THISTLE COCKTAIL.	2 Dashes Angostura Bitters. ½ Italian Vermouth. ½ Scotch Whisky. *Shake well and strain into cocktail glass.*
THREE MILLER COCKTAIL.	1 Teaspoonful Grenadine. 1 Dash Lemon Juice. ⅔ Brandy. ⅓ Bacardi Rum. *Shake well and strain into cocktail glass.*
THREE STRIPES COCKTAIL.	3 Slices Orange. ⅓ French Vermouth. ⅔ Dry Gin. *Shake well and strain into cocktail glass.*
THUNDER COCKTAIL.	1 Teaspoonful Gomme Syrup. The Yolk of 1 Egg. 1 Glass Brandy. 1 Sprinkle of Cayenne Pepper. *Shake well and strain into cocktail glass.*
THUNDER AND LIGHTNING COCKTAIL.	The Yolk of 1 Egg. 1 Teaspoonful Powdered Sugar. 1 Glass Brandy. *Shake well and strain into medium size glass. Dash of Cayenne Pepper on top.*

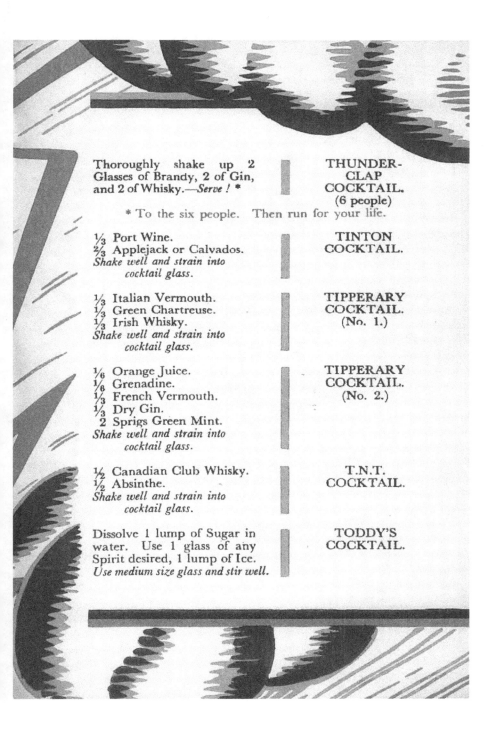

Thoroughly shake up 2 Glasses of Brandy, 2 of Gin, and 2 of Whisky.—*Serve!* * * To the six people. Then run for your life.	THUNDER-CLAP COCKTAIL. (6 people)
1/3 Port Wine. 2/3 Applejack or Calvados. *Shake well and strain into cocktail glass.*	TINTON COCKTAIL.
1/3 Italian Vermouth. 1/3 Green Chartreuse. 1/3 Irish Whisky. *Shake well and strain into cocktail glass.*	TIPPERARY COCKTAIL. (No. 1.)
1/6 Orange Juice. 1/6 Grenadine. 1/3 French Vermouth. 1/3 Dry Gin. 2 Sprigs Green Mint. *Shake well and strain into cocktail glass.*	TIPPERARY COCKTAIL. (No. 2.)
1/2 Canadian Club Whisky. 1/2 Absinthe. *Shake well and strain into cocktail glass.*	T.N.T. COCKTAIL.
Dissolve 1 lump of Sugar in water. Use 1 glass of any Spirit desired, 1 lump of Ice. *Use medium size glass and stir well.*	TODDY'S COCKTAIL.

COCKTAILS

TOM AND JERRY.*
- 1 Egg.
- ½ Glass Jamaica Rum.
- 1 Tablespoonful Powdered Sugar.
- ½ Glass Brandy.

Beat up yolk and white of egg separately. Then mix the yolk and white together.

Use stem glass or china mug, adding the spirits, then fill with boiling water, grating nutmeg on top.

* The *Tom and Jerry* was invented by Professor Jerry Thomas—rise please—over seventy years ago, in the days when New York was the scene of the soundest drinking on earth. The *Tom and Jerry* and the *Blue Blazer*—the latter a powerful concoction of burning whisky and boiling water—were the greatest cold weather beverages of that era.

TORPEDO COCKTAIL.
- 1 Dash Gin.
- ⅓ Brandy.
- ⅔ Calvados.

Shake well and strain into cocktail glass.

TRANSVAAL COCKTAIL.
- 3 Dashes Orange Bitters.
- ½ Gin. ½ Caperitif.

Stir well and strain into cocktail glass.

TRILBY COCKTAIL. (No. 1.)
- 2 Dashes Orange Bitters
- ½ Italian Vermouth.
- ½ Dry Gin.

Shake well and strain into cocktail glass.

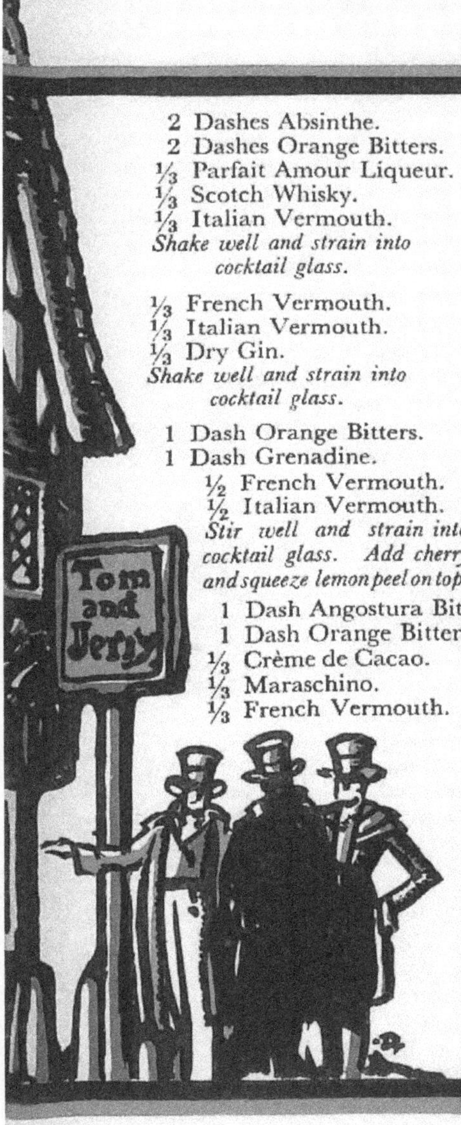

COCKTAILS

2 Dashes Absinthe.
2 Dashes Orange Bitters.
⅓ Parfait Amour Liqueur.
⅓ Scotch Whisky.
⅓ Italian Vermouth.
*Shake well and strain into
    cocktail glass.*

**TRILBY
COCKTAIL.
(No. 2.)**

⅓ French Vermouth.
⅓ Italian Vermouth.
⅓ Dry Gin.
*Shake well and strain into
    cocktail glass.*

**TRINITY
COCKTAIL**

1 Dash Orange Bitters.
1 Dash Grenadine.
    ½ French Vermouth.
    ½ Italian Vermouth.
*Stir well and strain into
cocktail glass. Add cherry
and squeeze lemon peel on top.*

**TROCADERO
COCKTAIL.**

1 Dash Angostura Bitters.
1 Dash Orange Bitters.
⅓ Crème de Cacao.
⅓ Maraschino.
⅓ French Vermouth.

**TROPICAL
COCKTAIL.**

*Shake well and strain
    into cocktail glass.*

TULIP COCKTAIL.
⅙ Lemon Juice.
⅙ Apricot Brandy.
⅓ Italian Vermouth.
⅓ Calvados or Apple
    Brandy.
*Shake well and strain into
    cocktail glass.*

COCKTAILS

TURF COCKTAIL.

2 Dashes Orange Bitters.
2 Dashes Maraschino.
2 Dashes Absinthe.
½ French Vermouth.
½ Plymouth Gin.
Shake well and strain into cocktail glass.

TUXEDO COCKTAIL. (No. 1.)

1 Piece Lemon Peel.
2 Dashes Absinthe.
½ French Vermouth.
½ Dry Gin.
Shake well and strain into cocktail glass.

TUXEDO COCKTAIL. (No. 2.)

1 Dash Maraschino.
1 Dash Absinthe.
2 Dashes Orange Bitters.
½ Dry Gin.
½ French Vermouth.
Shake well and strain into cocktail glass. Add a cherry. Squeeze lemon peel on top.

TWELVE MILES OUT COCKTAIL.

⅓ Bacardi Rum.
⅓ Swedish Punch.
⅓ Calvados.
Shake well and strain into cocktail glass. Squeeze orange peel on top.

TWIN SIX COCKTAIL

1 Dash Grenadine.
4 Dashes Orange Juice.
The White of 1 Egg.
¼ Italian Vermouth.
¾ Dry Gin.
Shake well and strain into medium size glass.

COCKTAILS

1 Dash Absinthe.
⅓ Cointreau.
⅔ Dry Gin.
*Shake well and strain into
cocktail glass.*

**ULANDA
COCKTAIL**

⅓ Grenadine.
⅓ Maraschino.
½ Green Chartreuse.
*Use liqueur glass and pour in-
gredients carefully so that they do
not mix.*

UNION JACK.

The Juice of ¼ Lemon.
1 Glass Dubonnet.
*Use medium size glass and fill
with soda water.*

**UPSTAIRS
COCKTAIL.**

2 Dashes Grand Marnier.
2 Dashes Angostura Bitters.
½ Sherry.
½ Canadian Club Whisky.
*Shake well and strain into
cocktail glass.*

**UP-TO-DATE
COCKTAIL.**

4 Dashes Orange Bitters.
⅓ Orange Juice.
⅔ Apricot Brandy.
*Shake well and strain into
cocktail glass.*

**VALENCIA
COCKTAIL.
(No. 1.)**

4 Dashes Orange Bitters.
⅓ Orange Juice.
⅔ Apricot Brandy.
*Shake well, strain into medium
size glass, and fill with Champagne.*

**VALENCIA
COCKTAIL.
(No. 2.)**

VANDERBILT COCKTAIL.

3 Dashes Syrup.
2 Dashes Angostura Bitters.
¼ Cherry Brandy.
¾ Brandy.
Shake well and strain into cocktail glass.

VAN DUSEN COCKTAIL.

2 Dashes Grand Marnier.
⅓ French Vermouth.
⅔ Dry Gin.
Shake well and strain into cocktail glass.

VELOCITY COCKTAIL

⅓ Dry Gin.
⅔ Italian Vermouth.
1 Slice of Orange.
Shake well and strain into cocktail glass.

VERMOUTH COCKTAIL.
1 Glass Italian or French Vermouth.
4 Dashes Orange or 1 Dash Angostura Bitters.
Stir well and strain into cocktail glass.

VERMOUTH AND CASSIS COCKTAIL.
1 Glass French Vermouth.
1 Liqueur Glass Crème de Cassis.
Use medium size glass and fill with soda water.

VERMOUTH AND CURAÇAO COCKTAIL.
1 Glass French Vermouth.
½ Liqueur Glass Curaçao.
Use medium size glass and fill with soda water.

VICTOR COCKTAIL.
¼ Brandy.
½ Italian Vermouth.
¼ Dry Gin.
Shake well and strain into cocktail glass.

VICTORY COCKTAIL.
½ Grenadine.
½ Absinthe.
Shake well, strain into medium size glass, and fill with soda water.

COCKTAILS

VIE ROSE COCKTAIL.

⅙ Lemon Juice. ⅙ Grenadine.
⅓ Dry Gin. ⅓ Kirsch.
Shake well and strain into cocktail glass.

VICTOR COCKTAIL.

½ Italian Vermouth.
¼ Dry Gin. ¼ Brandy.
Shake well and strain into cocktail glass.

VIRGIN COCKTAIL.

⅓ Forbidden Fruit Liqueur.
⅓ White Crème de Menthe.
⅓ Dry Gin.
Shake well and strain into cocktail glass.

VIRGIN SPECIAL COCKTAIL.
(6 people)

Take a glassful of red-currant juice, and a half glass of gooseberry syrup. In another vessel bruise a glassful of fresh raspberries, upon which pour successively a glass of Brandy, 2 glasses of Gin, then the currant juice and gooseberry syrup, and let stand for half an hour. Then add a glass of White Wine, the ice, and shake.
Serve, placing in the glasses either a raspberry or a small sprig of red-currants.

A very pleasant and refreshing summer cocktail.

VOLSTEAD COCKTAIL.

¼ Lime Juice.
¾ Orange Juice.
1 Dash of Hercules.
Shake well and strain into cocktail glass.

COCKTAILS

1 Teaspoonful Chartreuse.
⅓ Italian Vermouth.
⅓ Dry Gin.
⅓ Calvados or Apple Brandy.
*Shake well and strain into
    cocktail glass.*

**WARDAY'S
COCKTAIL.**

1 Teaspoonful Grenadine.
¼ Orange Juice.
¼ Lemon Juice.
½ Rye Whisky.
*Shake well and strain into
    cocktail glass.*

**WARD EIGHT
COCKTAIL.**

¼ French Vermouth.
¼ Hercules.
½ Dry Gin.
*Shake well and strain into
    cocktail glass.*

**WARDEN
COCKTAIL.**

½ Liqueur Glass Chartreuse.
½ Brandy.
*Use cocktail glass. 1 piece of
Peel in glass to form a circle.
Fill with cracked ice. Pour the
liquors very carefully so that
they do not mix. Brandy must
    be poured in last.*

**WARD'S
COCKTAIL.**

The Juice of ¼ Lemon or
    ½ Lime.
¼ Dry Gin.
½ Swedish Punch.
*Shake well and strain into
    cocktail glass.*

**WALDORF
COCKTAIL.**

A WEDDING BELLE COCKTAIL.

COCKTAILS

2 Dashes Angostura Bitters.
2 Dashes Syrup.
⅔ French Vermouth.
⅓ Brandy.
Shake well and strain into
cocktail glass.

WASHINGTON COCKTAIL.

2 Dashes Grenadine.
½ Teaspoonful   Powdered
Sugar.
The Juice of ¼ Lemon or
½ Lime.
The White of 1 Egg.
1 Glass Brandy.
Shake well and strain into
cocktail glass.
* *Yes*, Sir !   A stem-winder.

WATERBURY* COCKTAIL.

3 Dashes Orange Bitters.
1 Glass Plymouth Gin.
Shake well and strain into
cocktail glass.

WAX COCKTAIL.

⅛ Lime Juice.
⅛ Apricot Brandy.
¼ French Vermouth.
½ Plymouth Gin.
Shake well and strain into
cocktail glass.

WEBSTER COCKTAIL.

A favourite cocktail at the Bar of the S.S.
Mauretania.

⅙ Orange Juice.
⅙ Cherry Brandy.
⅓ Dry Gin.   ⅓ Dubonnet.
Shake well and strain into
cocktail glass.

WEDDING BELLE COCKTAIL.

COCKTAILS

WEESUER SPECIAL COCKTAIL.

4 Dashes Absinthe.
¼ French Vermouth.
¼ Italian Vermouth.
¼ Orange Curaçao.
¼ Dry Gin.
Shake well and strain into cocktail glass.

WELCOME STRANGER COCKTAIL.

⅙ Grenadine.
⅙ Lemon Juice.
⅙ Orange Juice.
⅙ Gin.
⅙ Cederlund's Swedish Punch.
⅙ Brandy.
Shake well and strain into cocktail glass.

WEMBLEY COCKTAIL. (No. 1.)

1 Dash Apricot Brandy.
2 Dashes Calvados.
⅓ French Vermouth.
⅔ Dry Gin.
Shake well and strain into cocktail glass.

WEMBLEY COCKTAIL. (No. 2.)

⅓ Scotch Whisky.
⅓ French Vermouth.
⅓ Pineapple Juice.
Shake well and strain into cocktail glass.

WESTBROOK COCKTAIL. (6 people)

3½ Glasses Gin.
1½ Glasses Italian Vermouth.
1 Glass Whisky.
Before shaking, add a little castor sugar.

COCKTAILS

1 Dash Lemon Juice.
¼ French Vermouth.
¼ Apricot Brandy.
½ Dry Gin.
*Shake well and strain into
cocktail glass.*

**WESTERN
ROSE
COCKTAIL.**

1 Teaspoonful Sugar in
    medium-sized Tumbler.
4 Dashes Angostura.
1 Teaspoonful Lemon Juice.
1 Glass Burrough's Beef-
    eater Gin.
1 Lump of Ice.
Stir and serve in same glass.

**WEST
INDIAN
COCKTAIL.**

⅓ Absinthe. ⅓ Anisette.
⅓ Brandy.
*Shake well and strain into
cocktail glass.*

**WHICH WAY
COCKTAIL.**

1 Dash Absinthe.
3 Dashes Curaçao.
¼ French Vermouth.
¼ Italian Vermouth.
½ Brandy.
*Shake well and strain into
cocktail glass.*

**WHIP
COCKTAIL.**

1 Dash Angostura Bitters.
4 Dashes Syrup.
1 Glass Canadian Club
    Whisky.
*Stir well and strain in cocktail
glass. Add a cherry.*

**WHISKY
COCKTAIL.**

WHISKY
SPECIAL
COCKTAIL.
(6 people)

3 Glasses Whisky.
2 Glasses French Vermouth.
½ Glass Orange Juice.
Pour into the shaker and shake, adding a little nutmeg. Serve with an olive. This is a very dry cocktail.

WHISPER
COCKTAIL.
(6 people)

2 Glasses Whisky.
2 Glasses French Vermouth.
2 Glasses Italian Vermouth.
Pour into a shaker half full of cracked ice. Shake well and serve.

This cocktail is very simple to make and is a great favourite in the West Indies.

WHIST
COCKTAIL.

¼ Bacardi Rum.
¼ Italian Vermouth.
½ Calvados.
Shake well and strain into cocktail glass.

This is a delightful drink that has been known in the West Indies for countless years. It might be described as a West Indies " Sundowner."

WHITE
BABY
COCKTAIL.

½ Gin. ¼ Cointreau.
¼ Sirop-de-Citron.
Shake well and strain into cocktail glass.

Some people substitute ink for the Gin and liquid blacking for the Cointreau and call it a Black Baby. But this is not advised.

COCKTAILS

½ Vanilla Ice Cream.
½ Gin.
No ice is necessary ; just shake until thoroughly mixed, and add water or white wine if the concoction is too thick.

THE WHITE CARGO COCKTAIL.

2 Dashes Orange Bitters.
2 Teaspoonsful Anisette.
1 Glass Dry Gin.
Stir well and strain into cocktail glass. Squeeze lemon peel on top.

WHITE COCKTAIL.

¼ Lemon Juice.
¼ Cointreau.
½ Dry Gin.
Shake well and strain into cocktail glass.

WHITE LADY COCKTAIL.

COCKTAILS

WHITE LILY COCKTAIL	⅓ Cointreau. ⅓ Bacardi Rum. ⅓ Gin 1 Dash Absinthe. *Shake well and strain into cocktail glass.*
WHITE PLUSH COCKTAIL.	1 Glass Dry Gin. 1 Liqueur Glass Maraschino. ½ Pint of Milk. *Shake well and strain into long tumbler.*
WHITE ROSE COCKTAIL.	The Juice of ¼ Orange. The Juice of ¼ Lemon or ½ Lime. The White of 1 Egg. ¼ Maraschino. ¾ Dry Gin. *Shake well and strain into medium size glass.*
WHITE WINGS COCKTAIL.	⅓ White Crème de Menthe. ⅔ Dry Gin. *Shake well and strain into cocktail glass.*
WHIZZ-DOODLE COCKTAIL.	¼ Scotch Whisky. ¼ Sweet Cream. ¼ Crème de Cacao. ¼ Dry Gin *Shake well and strain into cocktail glass.*

COCKTAILS

2 Dashes Absinthe.
2 Dashes Grenadine.
2 Dashes Orange Bitters.
⅓ French Vermouth.
⅔ Scotch Whisky.
*Shake well and strain into
    cocktail glass.*

**WHIZZ-
BANG
COCKTAIL.**

1 Egg.
1 Liqueur Glass Bénédictine.
*Shake well. strain into medium
size glass, and fill glass with
        Cream.*

**WIDOW'S
DREAM
COCKTAIL.**

1 Dash Angostura Bitters.
½ Liqueur Glass Chartreuse.
½ Liqueur Glass Bénédictine.
1 Liqueur Glass Calvados
        or Apple Brandy.
*Shake well and strain into
    cocktail glass.*

**WIDOW'S
KISS
COCKTAIL.**

1 Dash Lemon Juice.
⅓ Maraschino. ⅔ Brandy.
*Shake well and strain into
    cocktail glass.*

**WILLIE
SMITH
COCKTAIL.**

¼ Orange Juice.
¼ French Vermouth.
½ Plymouth Gin.
4 Dashes Curaçao.
*Shake well and strain into
    cocktail glass.*

**WILL
ROGERS
COCKTAIL.**

1 Glass Blackberry Brandy.
*Shake well and strain into cock-
tail glass.   A little nutmeg on
            top.*

**WINDY
CORNER
COCKTAIL.**

COCKTAILS

WOW COCKTAIL.

¼ Bacardi Rum.
¼ Hercules.
¼ Calvados or Apple Brandy.
¼ Brandy.
Shake well and strain into cocktail glass.

WYOMING SWING COCKTAIL.

The Juice of ¼ Orange.
½ Teaspoonful Powdered Sugar.
½ French Vermouth.
½ Italian Vermouth.
Shake well and strain into medium size glass, and fill with soda water.

XANTHIA COCKTAIL.

⅓ Cherry Brandy.
⅓ Yellow Chartreuse.
⅓ Dry Gin.
Shake well and strain into cocktail glass.

XERES COCKTAIL.

1 Dash Orange Bitters.
1 Dash Peach Bitters.
1 Glass Sherry.
Stir well and strain into cocktail glass.

X.Y.Z. COCKTAIL.

¼ Lemon Juice.
¼ Cointreau.
½ Bacardi Rum.
Shake well and strain into cocktail glass.

COCKTAILS

3 Dashes Orange Bitters.
1 Dash Angostura Bitters.
1 Glass Dry Gin.
Shake well and strain into small glass. Add a little syphon and squeeze lemon peel on top.

YALE COCKTAIL.

2 Glasses Gin.
2 Glasses French Vermouth.
1 Glass Grand Marnier.
Before shaking add a dash of Absinthe.

YELLOW DAISY COCKTAIL.*
(6 people)

* Not only the favourite drink, but also the one made famous, if not invented, by Richard William (" Deadwood Dick ") Clark, recently deceased (84) : onetime Custer Scout, Pony Express rider, Deadwood Gulch stage-coach guard, inspiration for all the (64) *Deadwood Dick* novels of E. L. Wheeler ; friend of Wild Westerners, Wild Bill Hickok, Buffalo Bill, Poker Alice Tubbs, Calamity Jane, Madame Mustache and Diamond Dick Turner of Norfolk, Neb. : Clark is buried on Sunrise Mountain, overlooking Deadwood Gulch, S. Dak.

⅓ Absinthe.
⅓ Yellow Chartreuse.
⅓ Apricot Brandy.
Shake well and strain into cocktail glass.

YELLOW PARROT COCKTAIL.

¼ Orange Juice.
¼ French Vermouth.
¼ Italian Vermouth.
¼ Dry Gin.
Shake well and strain into cocktail glass, with small crushed pickled onion.

YELLOW RATTLER COCKTAIL.

COCKTAILS

YODEL COCKTAIL.

½ Orange Juice.
½ Fernet Branca.
*Use medium size glass, and fill
with soda water.*

YOKOHAMA COCKTAIL.

1 Dash Absinthe.
⅙ Grenadine.
⅙ Vodka. ⅓ Orange Juice.
⅓ Dry Gin.
*Shake well and strain into
cocktail glass.*

YOLANDA COCKTAIL.

1 Dash Grenadine.
1 Dash Absinthe.
¼ Dry Gin.
½ Italian Vermouth.
¼ Brandy.
*Shake well and strain into
cocktail glass.*

YORK SPECIAL COCKTAIL.

4 Dashes Orange Bitters.
¼ Maraschino.
¾ French Vermouth.
*Shake well and strain into
cocktail glass.*

YOUNG MAN COCKTAIL.

1 Dash Angostura Bitters.
2 Dashes Curaçao.
¼ Italian Vermouth.
¾ Brandy.
*Shake well and strain into cock-
tail glass. Add olive or cherry.*

COCKTAILS

The Juice of 1½ Lemons.
1 Glass Gin.
3 Glasses French Vermouth.
1 or 2 Dessertspoonsful
    Sugar Syrup.
If desired, 1 Spoonful
    Orange Bitters.
*Shake well and serve with a
piece of lemon rind.*

**ZANZIBAR
COCKTAIL**
(6 people)

½ Dubonnet.
½ Dry Gin.
*Shake well and strain into
cocktail glass.*

**ZAZA
COCKTAIL.**

⅙ Bacardi Rum.
⅙ Anisette.
⅙ Gomme Syrup.
⅓ Canadian Club Whisky
1 Dash Angostura Bitters
1 Dash Orange Bitters.
3 Dashes Absinthe
*Shake well and strain into cock-
tail glass. Squeeze lemon peel.
on top.*

**ZAZARAC
COCKTAIL.**

½ Hercules.
½ Calvados or Apple Brandy.
*Shake well and strain into
cocktail glass.*

**ZED
COCKTAIL.**

END
OF THE
COCKTAILS.

COCKTAILS

PREPARED COCKTAILS FOR BOTTLING.

GIN COCKTAIL.

5 Gallons Gin.
2 Gallons Water.
1 Quart Gomme Syrup.
2 Ounces Tincture of Orange
  Peel.
7 Ounces Tincture of Gentian.
½ Ounce Tincture of
  Cardamoms.
½ Ounce Tincture of
  Lemon Peel.

Mix together, and give the desired colour with Solferino and caramel, in equal proportions.

BOURBON COCKTAIL.

5 Gallons Bourbon Rye
  Whisky.
2 Gallons Water.
1 Quart Gomme Syrup.
2 Ounces Tincture of
  Orange Peel.
1 Ounce Tincture of
  Lemon Peel.
1 Ounce Tincture of
  Gentian.
½ Ounce Tincture of
  Cardamoms.

Mix these ingredients thoroughly and colour with Solferino and caramel, in equal proportions.

COCKTAILS

5 Gallons Strong Brandy.
2 Gallons Water.
1 Quart Bitters.
1 Quart Gomme Syrup.
1 Bottle Curaçao.
Mix thoroughly, and filter through Canton flannel.

BRANDY COCKTAIL.

5 Gallons Brandy.
2 Gallons Water.
1 Quart Gomme Syrup.
¼ Pint Essence of Cognac.
1 Ounce Tincture of Cloves.
1 Ounce Tincture of Gentian.
2 Ounces Tincture of Orange Peel.
¼ Ounce Tincture of Cardamoms.
½ Ounce Tincture of Liquorice Root.
Mix the essence and tinctures with a portion of the spirits ; add the remainder of the ingredients, and colour with a sufficient quantity of Solferino and caramel (in equal parts) to give the desired colour.

BRANDY COCKTAIL
(Another recipe)

COCKTAILS

NON-ALCOHOLIC COCKTAILS.

CLAYTON'S PUSSYFOOT COCKTAIL.

¼ Sirop-de-Citron.
¼ Orange Juice.
½ Kola Tonic.
Shake well and serve in cocktail glass

CLAYTON'S TEMPERANCE COCKTAIL.

¼ Sirop-de-Citron.
¾ Kola Tonic.
Shake well and serve in cocktail glass.

KEEP SOBER COCKTAIL.

⅛ Grenadine.
⅛ Sirop-de-Citron.
¾ Tonic.
Serve in long glass and fill with siphon soda.

PARSON'S SPECIAL COCKTAIL.

4 Dashes Grenadine.
1 Glass Orange Juice.
The Yolk of 1 Egg.
Shake well and strain into medium size glass.

COCKTAILS SUITABLE FOR A PROHIBITION COUNTRY.

The following cocktails are especially suitable for those countries where they make the best of Prohibition, and where the ingredients for making them are obtainable without much difficulty.

¼ White Grape Juice.
4 Dashes Grenadine or Syrup.
¾ Scotch Whisky
Shake well and strain into cocktail glass.

KARL K. KITCHEN COCKTAIL.

Crush 1 Lump of Sugar in a little water.
Crush 4 Leaves of Fresh Green Mint.
1 Dash Lemon Juice.
4 Dashes Orange Juice.
1 Glass Gin.
Shake well and strain into cocktail glass.

MR. MANHATTAN COCKTAIL.

Saturate 1 lump of Sugar with Raspberry Syrup or Grenadine.
⅓ Vermouth.
⅔ Hooch Whisky.
Shake well and strain into cocktail glass.

OH HARRY! COCKTAIL.

1 Dash Absinthe.
½ Applejack.
½ Brandy.
Shake well and strain into cocktail glass

SPECIAL (ROUGH) COCKTAIL.

SOURS AND TODDIES

SOURS.

A Sour is usually prepared from the following recipe :
The Juice of ½ Lemon.
½ Tablespoonful of Sugar.
Add 1 Glass of Spirit or Liqueur as fancy dictates, Gin, Whisky, Brandy, Rum, Calvados, etc.
Shake well and strain into medium size glass. One squirt of Soda water. Add one slice of orange and a cherry.

EGG SOUR.

1 Teaspoonful of Powdered White Sugar.
3 Dashes of Lemon Juice.
1 Liqueur Glass of Curaçao.
1 Liqueur Glass of Brandy.
1 Egg.
2 or 3 small Lumps of Ice.
Shake well and remove the ice before serving.

TODDIES.

WHISKY TODDY.

1 Teaspoonful of Sugar.
½ Wineglass of Water.
1 Wineglass of Whisky.
1 Small Lump of Ice.
Stir with a spoon, and serve.

BRANDY TODDY.

Dissolve 1 Lump of Sugar.
1 Lump of Ice.
1 Glass of Brandy.
Use medium size glass.

FLIPS

1 Teaspoonful of Powdered
     Sugar.
¼ Baked Apple.
1 Glass Calvados or Applejack.
Use stem glass and fill with
Boiling Water. Grate nutmeg
       on top.

**APPLE
TODDY.**

FLIPS.

The Flip, particularly the variety made with
Rum, is renowned as an old-fashioned drink of
great popularity among sailors.   It is usually
made in the following manner :—

1 Egg.
½ Tablespoon of Powdered
     Sugar.
1 Glass of Rum, Brandy,
     Port Wine, Sherry,
     or Whisky.

RUM FLIP.

Shake well and strain into medium size glass. Grate a
little nutmeg on top.   In cold weather a dash of Jamaica
Ginger can be added.

ALE FLIP.

Put on the fire in a saucepan one quart of Ale, and
let it boil ; have ready the whites of two eggs and
the yolks of four, well beaten up separately ; add
them by degrees to four tablespoonsful of moist
sugar, and half a nutmeg grated.   When all are
well mixed, pour on the boiling Ale by degrees,
beating up the mixture continually ; then pour
it rapidly backward and forward from one jug to
another, keeping one jug raised high above the
other ; till the flip is smooth and finely frothed.
This is a good remedy to take at the commencement
of a cold.

EGG NOGGS

EGG NOGGS.

The Egg Nogg is essentially an American Beverage, although it has been appreciated throughout the world for many years. Its introduction throughout Christmas time in the Southern States of America is traditional. In Scotland it is known as "Auld Man's Milk."

EGG NOGG.

1 Egg.
1 Tablespoonful Powdered Sugar.
1 Glass of any Spirit.desired.
Fill glass with Milk.
Shake well and strain into long tumbler. Grate a little nutmeg on top.

BALTIMORE EGG NOGG.

1 Fresh Egg.
½ Tablespoonful Sugar.
¼ Glass Brandy.
¼ Glass Jamaica Rum.
½ Glass Madeira.
½ Pint Fresh Milk.
Shake well and strain into long tumbler. Grate nutmeg on top.

BREAKFAST EGG NOGG.

1 Fresh Egg.
¼ Curaçao.
¾ Brandy.
¼ Pint Fresh Milk.
Shake well and strain into long tumbler. Grate nutmeg on top.

TOM COLLINS

1 Egg.
1½ Teaspoonsful of Sugar.
2 or 3 Small Lumps of Ice.
Fill the tumbler with Cider, and shake well.

GENERAL HARRISON'S EGG NOGG.

This is a splendid drink, and is very popular on the Mississippi river. It was the favourite beverage of William Henry Harrison, ninth President of the United States of America.

TOM COLLINS.

The Juice of ½ Lemon.
½ Tablespoonful Powdered Sugar.
1 Glass Dry Gin.
Shake well and strain into long tumbler. Add 1 lump ice and split of soda water.

TOM COLLINS.

5 or 6 Dashes of Gomme Syrup.
The Juice of 1 Small Lemon.
1 Large Wineglass Whisky.
2 or 3 Lumps of Ice.
Use small bar glass.
Shake well and strain into a large bar glass. Fill up the glass with plain soda water and imbibe while it is lively.

TOM COLLINS WHISKY.

SLINGS

JOHN COLLINS.

The Juice of ½ Lemon.
½ Tablespoonful Powdered
Sugar.
1 Glass Hollands Gin.
*Shake well and strain into
long tumbler. Add 1 lump ice
and split of soda water.*

SLINGS.

GIN SLING.

Dissolve 1 Teaspoonful of
Sugar in Water.
1 Glass Dry Gin.
1 Lump of Ice.
*Served in long tumbler and fill
with water or soda ; if served
hot a little nutmeg on top.*

SINGAPORE SLING.

The Juice of ¼ Lemon.
¼ Dry Gin.
½ Cherry Brandy.
*Shake well and strain into
medium size glass, and fill with
soda water. Add 1 lump of ice.*

**STRAITS SLING.
(6 people)**

Place in a shaker 4
glasses of Gin, 1 glass
of Bénédictine, 1 glass of
Cherry Brandy, the Juice
of 2 Lemons, a teaspoonful of
Angostura Bitters, and one of
Orange Bitters.
*Shake sufficiently, and serve in
large glasses, filling up with
Soda water.*

SHRUBS

BRANDY SHRUB.

To the thin rinds of 2 Lemons and the juice of 5, add 2 quarts of Brandy ; cover it for 3 days, then add a quart of Sherry and 2 pounds of loaf Sugar, run it through a jelly bag and bottle it.

RUM SHRUB.

Put 3 pints of Orange Juice and 1 pound of loaf Sugar to a gallon of Rum. Put all into a cask, and leave it for 6 weeks, when it will be ready for use.

CURRANT SHRUB.

1 Pint of Sugar.
1 Pint of Strained Currant Juice.
Boil it gently for eight or ten minutes, skimming it well ; take it off and, when luke-warm, add half a gill of Brandy to every pint of Shrub. Bottle tight.

WHITE CURRANT SHRUB.

Strip the fruit, and prepare in a jar, as for jelly ; strain the juice, of which put two quarts to 1 gallon of Rum, and 2 pounds of Lump Sugar; strain through a jelly bag.

SANGAREES.

SAVOY SANGAREE.

1 Teaspoonful Powdered Sugar.
1 Glass of Sherry or Port.
Stir well and strain into medium size glass, add slice of orange or lemon peel, and a little nutmeg on top.

SHERRY SANGAREE.
Use small bar glass.

1 Wineglass of Sherry.
1 Teaspoonful of Fine Sugar.
Fill tumbler ⅓ with ice, and grate nutmeg on top.

PORT WINE SANGAREE.

1⅓ Wineglasses of Port Wine.
1 Teaspoonful of Sugar.
Fill tumbler ⅔ full of ice. Shake well and grate nutmeg on top.

HIGHBALLS.

Use medium size glass.
1 Lump of Ice.
1 Glass of any Spirit, Liqueur or Wine desired.
Fill glass with syphon soda water or split of soda. Ginger Ale can be used if preferred. Add twist of Lemon Peel if desired.

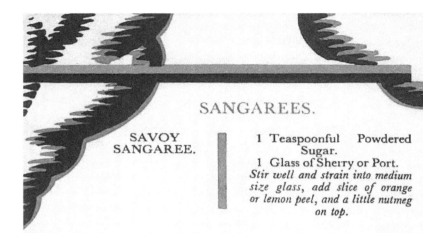
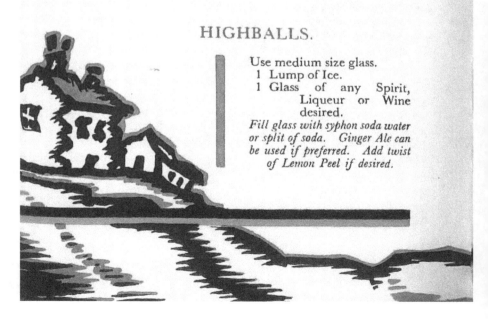

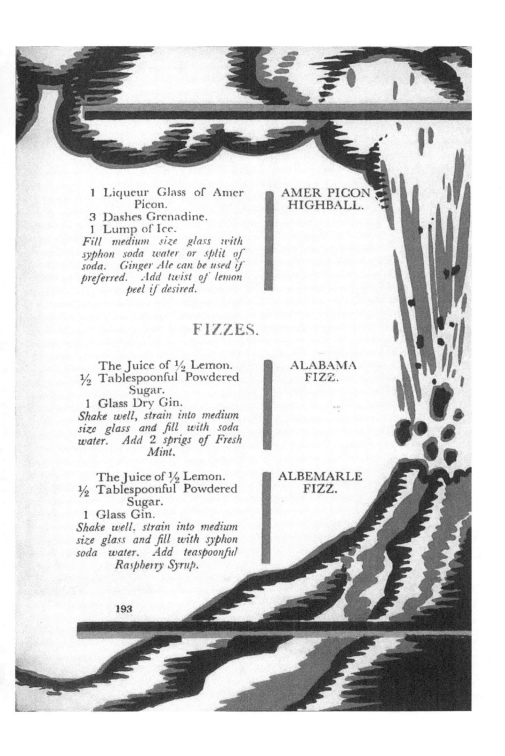

AMER PICON HIGHBALL.

1 Liqueur Glass of Amer Picon.
3 Dashes Grenadine.
1 Lump of Ice.
Fill medium size glass with syphon soda water or split of soda. Ginger Ale can be used if preferred. Add twist of lemon peel if desired.

FIZZES.

ALABAMA FIZZ.

The Juice of ½ Lemon.
½ Tablespoonful Powdered Sugar.
1 Glass Dry Gin.
Shake well, strain into medium size glass and fill with soda water. Add 2 sprigs of Fresh Mint.

ALBEMARLE FIZZ.

The Juice of ½ Lemon.
½ Tablespoonful Powdered Sugar.
1 Glass Gin.
Shake well, strain into medium size glass and fill with syphon soda water. Add teaspoonful Raspberry Syrup.

FIZZES

APPLE BLOW FIZZ.

The White of 1 Egg.
4 Dashes Lemon Juice.
1 Teaspoonful of Powdered Sugar.
1 Glass Calvados.
Shake well, strain into medium size glass and fill with soda water.

BRANDY FIZZ.

The Juice of ½ Lemon.
½ Tablespoonful Powdered Sugar.
1 Glass Brandy.
Shake well, strain into medium size glass and fill with syphon soda water.

BUCKS FIZZ.

Use long tumbler.
¼ Glass Orange Juice.
Fill with Champagne.

CREAM FIZZ.

The Juice of ½ Lemon.
½ Tablespoonful Powdered Sugar.
1 Glass Dry Gin.
1 Teaspoonful Fresh Cream.
Shake well, strain into medium size glass and fill with soda water.

FIZZES

5 Dashes Lemon Juice.
1 Teaspoonful of Powdered Sugar.
1 Egg.
1 Glass Canadian Club or Scotch Whisky.
3 Dashes Curaçao.
Shake well, strain into medium size glass and fill with soda water.

DERBY FIZZ.

The Juice of ½ Orange.
The Juice of ¼ Lemon.
1 Teaspoonful Cherry Brandy.
1 Glass Dubonnet.
Shake well, strain into medium size glass. Fill with soda water.

DUBONNET FIZZ.

The Juice of ½ Lemon.
½ Tablespoonful Powdered Sugar.
1 Glass Gin.
Shake well, strain into medium size glass and fill with syphon soda water.

GIN FIZZ.

FIZZES

GOLDEN FIZZ.

The Juice of ½ Lemon.
½ Tablespoonful Powdered
Sugar. 1 Glass Gin.
The Yolk of 1 Egg.
*Shake well, strain into medium
size glass and fill with syphon
soda water.*

GRAND ROYAL FIZZ.

The Juice of ½ Lemon.
½ Tablespoonful Powdered
Sugar. 1 Glass Gin.
2 Dashes Maraschino.
The Juice of ¼ Orange.
1 Tablespoonful Sweet
Cream.
*Shake well, strain into medium
size glass and fill with syphon
soda water.*

HOFFMANN FIZZ.

The Juice of ½ Lemon.
½ Tablespoonful Powdered
Sugar. 1 Glass Gin.
*Shake well, strain into medium
size glass and fill with syphon
soda water. Add teaspoonful of
Grenadine.*

HOLLAND FIZZ.

The Juice of ½ Lemon.
½ Tablespoonful Powdered
Sugar. 1 Glass Gin.
The White of 1 Egg.
*Shake well, strain into medium
size glass and fill with syphon
soda water. Add 3 sprigs of
fresh Mint.*

FIZZES

The Juice of ½ Lemon.
⅓ Rum.
⅔ Canadian Club or Scotch
Whisky.
½ Tablespoonful Sugar.
Shake well, strain into medium size glass and fill with syphon soda water.

IMPERIAL FIZZ.

1 Teaspoonful Grenadine.
The Juice of ½ Lemon.
1 Liqueur Glass Swedish
Punch.
Shake well, strain into medium size glass and fill with soda water.

MAY BLOSSOM FIZZ.

The Juice of ½ Lemon or
1 Lime.
½ Tablespoonful Powdered
Sugar.
The White of 1 Egg.
2 Dashes Absinthe.
1 Glass Scotch Whisky.
Shake well, strain into long tumbler and fill with syphon soda water.

MORNING GLORY FIZZ.

The Juice of ½ Lemon.
½ Tablespoonful Powdered
Sugar.
The White of 1 Egg.
1 Glass of Dry Gin.
3 Dashes Fleur d'Orange.
1 Tablespoonful of Sweet
Cream.
Shake well, strain into long tumbler and fill with syphon soda water.

NEW ORLEANS GIN FIZZ.

FIZZES

ORANGE FIZZ.

The Juice of ½ Orange.
The Juice of ¼ Lemon or ½ Lime.
1 Glass Dry Gin.
Shake well, strain into medium size glass and fill with syphon soda.

ORGEAT FIZZ.

The Juice of ½ Lemon.
1 Liqueur Glass Orgeat.
Shake well, strain into medium size glass and fill with soda water.

OSTEND FIZZ.

½ Liqueur Glass Crème de Cassis.
½ Liqueur Glass Kirsch.
Shake well, strain into medium size glass and fill with soda water.

FIZZES

The Juice of ½ Lemon or
   1 Lime.
4 Mashed Strawberries.
½ Tablespoonful Powdered
   Sugar.
1 Tablespoonful   Sweet
   Cream.
1 Glass Dry Gin.
*Shake well, strain into medium
size glass and fill with syphon
soda water.*

**PEACH
BLOW FIZZ.**

2 Tablespoonsful Pineapple
   Juice.
½ Tablespoonful Powdered
   Sugar.
1 Glass Bacardi Rum.
*Shake well, strain into medium
size glass and fill with syphon
soda water.*

**PINEAPPLE
FIZZ.**

The Juice of ½ Lemon.
½ Tablespoonful Powdered
   Sugar.
1 Glass Gin.
1 Egg.
*Shake well, strain into medium
size glass and fill with syphon
soda water.*

**ROYAL
FIZZ.**

FIZZES

RUBY FIZZ.

The Juice of ½ Lemon.
½ Tablespoonful Powdered Sugar.
The White of 1 Egg.
2 Dashes Raspberry or Grenadine Syrup.
1 Glass Sloe Gin.
Shake well, strain into medium size glass and fill with syphon soda water.

SILVER FIZZ.

The Juice of ½ Lemon.
½ Tablespoonful Powdered Sugar.
1 Glass Gin.
The White of 1 Egg.
Shake well, strain into medium size glass and fill with syphon soda water.

SOUTH SIDE FIZZ.

The Juice of ½ Lemon.
½ Tablespoonful Powdered Sugar.
1 Glass Gin.
Shake well, strain into medium size glass and fill with syphon soda water. Add fresh Mint leaves.

TEXAS FIZZ.

The Juice of ¼ Orange.
The Juice of ¼ Lemon.
1 Teaspoonful Powdered Sugar.
1 Glass Dry Gin.
Shake well, strain into medium size glass and fill with syphon soda water.

COOLERS.

APRICOT COOLER.

The Juice of ½ Lemon or 1 Lime.
2 Dashes Grenadine.
1 Liqueur Glass Apricot Brandy.
Shake well, strain into long tumbler and fill with soda water.

HARVARD COOLER.

The Juice of ½ Lemon or 1 Lime.
½ Tablespoonful Sugar.
1 Glass Applejack or Calvados.
Shake well, strain into long tumbler and fill with soda water.

HIGHLAND COOLER.

1 Teaspoonful Powdered Sugar.
The Juice of ½ Lemon.
2 Dashes Angostura Bitters.
1 Glass Scotch Whisky.
1 Lump of Ice.
Use long tumbler and fill with Ginger Ale.

LONE TREE COOLER.

The Juice of ¼ Lemon.
The Juice of 1 Orange.
⅓ French Vermouth.
⅔ Dry Gin.
1 Liqueur Glass Grenadine.
Shake well, strain into tumbler and fill with soda water.

COOLERS

LONG TOM COOLER.

The Juice of ½ Lemon.
½ Tablespoonful Sugar.
1 Glass Dry Gin.
Shake well, strain into long tumbler, add 1 lump of ice, and fill with soda water.

MANHATTAN COOLER.

The Juice of ½ Lemon or 1 Lime.
½ Tablespoonful Powdered Sugar.
1 Wineglass Claret.
3 Dashes Rum.
Stir well and strain into medium size glass. Decorate with fruit in season.

MINT COOLER.

1 Glass Scotch Whisky.
3 Dashes Crème de Menthe.
Use tumbler, 1 lump of Ice and fill with soda water.

MOONLIGHT COOLER

½ Tablespoonful Powdered Sugar.
The Juice of 1 Lemon.
1 Glass Calvados.
Shake well and strain into long tumbler. Fill with soda water and decorate with slices of fruit in season.

REMSEN COOLER.

1 Glass Dry Gin.
1 Split of Soda.
Peel rind of Lemon in spiral form, place in long tumbler with 1 lump of Ice, add Gin and fill with soda water.

RICKEYS

The Juice of ½ Lemon.
2 Dashes Grenadine.
½ Apricot Brandy.
½ Dry Gin.
1 Lump of Ice.
*Use long tumbler and fill with
soda Water.   2 sprigs of fresh
mint on top.*

**SEA BREEZE
COOLER.**

½ Tablespoonful of Sugar.
The Juice of ½ Lemon.
1 Glass Dry Gin.
*Use long tumbler, and fill with
Ginger Beer.*

**SHADY
GROVE
COOLER.**

RICKEYS.

Most Rickeys are made with the following recipe:—

Use medium size glass.
1 Lump of Ice.
  The Juice of ½ Lime of ¼
  Lemon.
  Then add 1 glass of any
  Spirit or Liqueur
  fancied — Whisky,
  Gin, Rum, Bourbon,
  Calvados, Caperitif,
  etc.
*Fill with Carbonated Water and
leave rind of Lime or Lemon in
glass.*

DAISIES

SAVOY HOTEL RICKEY.
Use medium size glass.
1 Lump of Ice.
The Juice of ½ Lime or ¼ Lemon.
1 Glass Gin. 4 Dashes Grenadine.
Fill with Carbonated Water and leave Rind of Lime or Lemon in glass.

DAISIES.

GIN DAISY.
The Juice of ½ Lemon.
¼ Tablespoonful Powdered Sugar.
6 Dashes Grenadine. 1 Glass Gin.
Use long tumbler. Half fill with cracked ice, stir until glass is frosted. Fill with Syphon Soda Water, put 4 sprigs of green mint on top and decorate with slices of fruit in season.

SANTA CRUZ RUM DAISY.
Use small bar glass.
3 or 4 Dashes Gomme Syrup.
2 or 3 Dashes Maraschino or Curaçao.
The Juice of ½ Small Lemon.
1 Wineglass Santa Cruz Rum.
Fill glass ⅓ full of shaved ice. Shake thoroughly, strain into a large cocktail glass, and fill up with Seltzer or Apollinaris Water.

FIXES

WHISKY DAISY.

Use small bar glass.
3 Dashes Gomme Syrup.
The Juice of ½ Small Lemon.
1 Wineglass Bourbon or Rye Whisky.
Fill glass ⅓ full of shaved ice. Shake thoroughly, strain into a large cocktail glass, and fill up with Apollinaris or Seltzer Water.

FIXES.

In making fixes be careful to put the lemon skin in the glass.

BRANDY FIX.

Pour into a small tumbler 1 teaspoonful of sugar, 1 teaspoonful of Water to dissolve the sugar, Juice of ½ Lemon, ½ Liqueur Glass of Cherry Brandy, 1 Liqueur Glass of Brandy.
Fill the glass with fine ice and stir slowly, then add a slice of lemon, and serve with a straw.

GIN FIX.

Use small bar glass.
1 Tablespoonful Sugar.
¼ Lemon.
½ Wineglass Water.
1 Wineglass Gin.
Fill ⅔ full of shaved ice. Stir with a spoon, and ornament the top with fruits in season.

JULEPS

SANTA CRUZ FIX.

The Santa Cruz fix is made by substituting Santa Cruz Rum for Brandy in the Brandy Fix.

WHISKY FIX.

1 Large Teaspoonful of Powdered White Sugar, dissolved in a little water.

The Juice of ½ Lemon.

1 Wineglass Bourbon or Rye Whisky.

Fill up the glass about ⅔ full of shaved ice, stir well, and ornament the top of the glass with fruit in season.

JULEPS.

MINT JULEPS.

The Julep is a delightful potion that originally came out of the Southern States of America, and many great men have sung its praises through the years. It was the famous Capt. Marryatt, skipper and novelist, who introduced the beverage into the British Isles, and below we quote his recipe in his own words :—

" I must descant a little upon the mint julep, as it is, with the thermometer at 100 degrees, one of the most delightful and insinuating potations that ever was invented, and may be drunk with equal satisfaction when the thermometer is as low as 70 degrees. There are many varieties, such as

those composed of Claret, Madeira, etc., but the ingredients of the real mint julep are as follows. I learned how to make them, and succeeded pretty well. Put into a tumbler about a dozen springs of the tender shoots of mint, upon them put a spoonful of white sugar, and equal proportions of Peach and common Brandy, so as to fill it up one-third, or perhaps a little less. Then take rasped or pounded ice, and fill up the tumbler. Epicures rub the lips of the tumbler with a piece of fresh pineapple, and the tumbler itself is very often incrusted outside with stalactites of ice. As the ice melts, you drink. I once overheard two ladies talking in the next room to me, and one of them said, ' Well, if I have a weakness for any one thing, it is for a mint julep ! '—a very amiable weakness, and proving her good sense and good taste. They are, in fact, like the American ladies, irresistible."

CHAMPAGNE JULEP.

Use long tumbler.
1 Lump Sugar.
2 Sprigs Mint.
Fill glass with Champagne. Stir gently and decorate with slices of fruit in season.

PINEAPPLE JULEP. (6 people)

Take a large glass jug and fill it ¼ full of crushed ice. Pour in the juice of two oranges, a glass of Raspberry Vinegar, a glass of Maraschino, a glass and a half of Gin, and a bottle of Sparkling Moselle or Saumur. Pull a pineapple to pieces with a silver fork and place the pieces in the jug. Stir the mixture, add a little fruit for appearance's sake, and serve.

SMASHES

SOUTHERN MINT JULEP.

4 Sprigs Fresh Mint.
½ Tablespoonful Powdered
Sugar.
1 Glass of Bourbon Rye, or
Canadian Club
Whisky.

Use long tumbler and crush the Mint leaves and dissolved sugar lightly together, add Spirits and fill glass with cracked ice ; stir gently until glass is frosted. Decorate on top with 3 Sprigs of Mint.

SMASHES.

The 'Smash' is in effect a Julep on a small plan. To prepare it the following recipe is usually used :—

Use medium sized glass.
Dissolve 1 Lump of Sugar.
Add 4 leaves of Green Mint, and crush Mint and
sugar very lightly together.
Place lump of ice in glass.
Then add one small glass of either Bacardi Rum,
Brandy, Gin, Irish Whisky, or Scotch
Whisky as fancy dictates.

Decorate with a slice of Orange, and squeeze Lemon peel on top.

COBBLERS AND FRAPPÉ

COBBLERS.

The cobbler is, like the Julep, a drink of American origin, although it is now an established favourite, particularly in warm climes. It is very easy to make, but it is usual to make it acceptable to the eye, as well as the palate, by decorating the glass after the ingredients are mixed. The usual recipe for preparing Cobblers is given below. To make a Whisky Cobbler substitute Whisky for Gin, For a Brandy Cobbler, substitute Brandy, and so on.

Fill glass half full with cracked ice.
Add 1 Teaspoonful of Powdered Sugar.
Add 1 Small Glass of Gin (or Whisky, or Brandy,
        as above).
Stir well, and decorate with slices of orange or pineapple.

FRAPPÉ.

$\frac{2}{3}$ Absinthe,
$\frac{1}{6}$ Syrup of Anisette, double
      quantity of water.
Shake up long enough until the outside of the shaker is thoroughly covered with ice. Strain into a small tumbler.

ABSINTHE FRAPPÉ.

PUNCHES

PUNCH.

" This ancient Silver bowl of mine, it tells
   of good old times,
Of joyous days, and jolly nights, and
   merry Christmas Chimes,
They were a free and jovial race, but honest,
   brave and true,
That dipped their ladle in the punch when
   this old bowl was new."

Thus runs the old drinking song by Oliver Wendell
Holmes, a song among many that have lauded the
old time jollity of Ye Punch Bowl.
The proper preparation of Punch requires considerable care, but there is one grand secret
in its concoction that must be mastered with
patience and care. It is just this, that the various
subtle ingredients be thoroughly mixed in such a
way, that neither the bitter, the sweet, the spirit,
nor any liquor be perceptible the one
over the other. This accomplishment
depends not so much upon the precise
proportions of the various elements, as
upon the order of their addition, and the
manner of mixing. Below are given a
selection of famous old Punch recipes
worthy of careful study.

BOMBAY PUNCH.

1 Qt. Brandy.
1 Qt. Sherry.
¼ Pt. Maraschino.
¼ Pt. Orange Curaçao.
4 Qts. Champagne.
2 Qts. Carbonated Water.

*Stir gently. Surround the Punch
Bowl with cracked ice and
decorate with fruits in
season.*

PUNCHES

The Juice of 15 Lemons.
The Juice of 4 Oranges.
1¼ lbs. Powdered Sugar.
½ Pt. Curaçao.
1 Glass Grenadine.
2 Qts. Brandy.
Place large block of ice in a punch bowl, add the above ingredients and from one to two quarts of sparkling water.

BRANDY PUNCH.

1½ lbs. Sugar.
2 Qts. Sparkling Water.
2 Qts. Claret.
1 Pt. Brandy.
1 Pt. Rum.
1 Pt. Sparkling White Wine.
1 Glass Italian Vermouth.
Use punch bowl with n large block of ice.

CARDINAL PUNCH.

½ lb. Powdered Sugar.
2 Qts. Champagne.
1 Qt. Mineral Water (Sparkling).
1 Glass Brandy.
1 Glass Maraschino.
1 Glass Curaçao.
Mix well in punch bowl. Surround bowl with cracked ice and add slices of fruit in season.

CHAMPAGNE PUNCH.

PUNCHES

CLARET PUNCH.

½ lb. Powdered Sugar.
3 Qts. Claret.
2 Qts. Sparkling Water.
½ Pt. Lemon Juice.
1 Glass Curaçao.
Mix well in punch bowl. Surround bowl with cracked ice. Add slices of fruits in season.

FISH HOUSE PUNCH.

The Juice of 6 Lemons.
½ lb. Powdered Sugar.
½ Pt. Brandy.
¼ Pt. Peach Brandy.
¼ Pt. Jamaica Rum.
3 Pts. Sparkling Water.
Use large punch bowl with block of ice.

GLASGOW PUNCH.

From a recipe in the possession of Dr. Shelton Mackenzie.

Melt lump sugar in cold water, with the juice of a couple of lemons, passed through a fine hairstrainer. This is the sherbet, and must be well mingled. Then add old Jamaica Rum—one part of Rum to five of sherbet. Cut a couple of limes in two, and run each section rapidly around the edge of the jug or bowl, gently squeezing in some of the delicate acid. This done, the Punch is made. Imbibe freely.

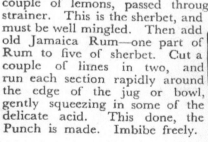

The Juice of 4 Lemons.
The Rind of 2 Lemons.
½ Pound of White Sugar, dissolved in just sufficient hot water.
1 Pineapple, peeled, sliced and pounded.
6 Cloves.
20 Coriander Seeds.
1 Small Stick Cinnamon.
1 Pint Brandy.
1 Pint Jamaica Rum.
1 Gill Batavia Arrack.
1 Cup Strong Green Tea.
1 Quart Boiling Water.
1 Quart Hot Milk.

**MILK PUNCH.
(No. 1.)**

Put all the materials in a clean demijohn, the boiling water to be added last; cork this down to prevent evaporation, and allow the ingredients to steep for at least six hours; then add the hot milk and the juice of two more lemons; mix and filter through a jelly-bag; and when the punch has passed bright, put it away in tightly corked bottles.

This punch is intended to be iced for drinking. If intended for immediate use, filtering is not necessary.

PUNCHES

MILK PUNCH (No. 2.)	1 Glass Milk. ½ Tablespoonful Powdered Sugar. 1 Glass Whisky or Rum. *Shake well and strain into long tumbler, grating a little nutmeg on top.*

NUREMBERG PUNCH.
(For a party of 15.)

Take ¾ of a pound of loaf sugar ; squeeze upon it, through muslin, the juice of two or more good-sized oranges ; add a little of the peel, cut very thin, pour upon a quart of boiling water, the third part of that quantity of Batavia Arrack, and a bottle of hot, but not boiling, Red or White French Wine—Red is best. Stir together. This is excellent when cold, and will improve with age.

OXFORD PUNCH.

Rub the rinds of three fresh lemons with loaf sugar, till you have extracted a portion of the juice ; finely cut the peel off two more lemons, and two sweet oranges. Add six glasses of calf's foot jelly ; let all be put into a large jug, and stir well together. Pour in two quarts of water boiling hot, and set the jug upon the hob for twenty minutes. Strain the liquor through a fine sieve into a large bowl ; put in a bottle of Capillaire, half a pint of Sherry, a pint of Cognac Brandy, a pint of old Jamaica Rum, and a quart of Orange Shrub ; stir well as you pour in the Spirit. If you find it requires more sweetness, add sugar to your taste.
As the pulp is disagreeable to some persons, the sherbet may be strained before the liquor is put in. Some strain the lemon before they put it to the

PUNCHES

sugar, which is improper, as, when the pulp and sugar are well mixed together, it adds much to the richness of the Punch.

When only Rum is used, about half a pint of Porter will soften the Punch ; and even when both Rum and Brandy are used, the Porter gives a richness, and to some a very pleasant flavour.

½ lb. Powdered Sugar.
3 Qts. Rhine Wine.
1 Qt. Sparkling Mineral Water.
1 Glass Brandy.
1 Glass Maraschino.
2 Tablespoonsful of Tea.

RHINE WINE PUNCH.
(10 persons).

Put the tea in a small piece of cheese cloth and leave in the above mixture for about ten minutes. Surround punch bowl with cracked ice and add slices of fruit in Season.

1 Qt. Champagne.
1 Qt. Rum.
½ Liqueur Glass Orange Bitters.
The Juice of 10 Lemons.
The Juice of 3 Oranges.
2 lbs. Sugar.
The Whites of 10 Eggs.

ROMAN PUNCH.

Use punch bowl. Dissolve Sugar in lemon and orange juice, add the rind of one orange, add the well beaten whites of eggs. Surround the bowl with cracked ice and stir the ingredients well together.

½ lb. Powdered Sugar.
2 Qts. Sauterne.
1 Liqueur Glass Maraschino.
1 Liqueur Glass Curaçao.
1 Liqueur Glass Grand Marnier.

SAUTERNE PUNCH.

Use punch bowl, 1 block of ice and add slices of fruit in season.

PUNCHES

UNCLE TOBY PUNCH.
ENGLISH.
(General Ford's Recipe.)

Take two large fresh lemons with rough skins, quite ripe, and some large lumps of double-refined sugar. Rub the sugar over the lemons till it has absorbed all the yellow part of the skins. Then put into the bowl these lumps, and as much more as the juice of the lemons may be supposed to require; for no certain weight can be mentioned as the acidity of a lemon cannot be known till tried, and therefore this must be determined by the taste. Then squeeze the lemon juice upon the sugar, and with a bruiser press the sugar and the juice particularly well together, for a great deal of the richness and fine flavour of the Punch depends on this rubbing and mixing process being thoroughly performed. Then mix this up very well with boiling water (soft water is best) till the whole is rather cool. When this mixture (which is now called the sherbet) is to your taste, take Brandy and Rum in equal quantities, and put them to it, mixing the whole well together again. The quantity of liquor must be according to your taste; two good lemons are generally enough to make four quarts of Punch, including a quart of liquor, with half a pound of sugar; but this depends much on taste, and on the strength of the Spirit.

PREPARED PUNCH FOR BOTTLING.

The advantages of having real Punch bottled, and therefore ready to hand at any time, will be immediately appreciated. To accomplish this, it is necessary to prepare the nectar in the form of a concentrated essence, the addition of hot or cold water being the only necessary step to produce a delectable Punch. Below will be found recipes to this end.

1½ Gallons Batavia Arrack.
3 Gallons Spirits.
3 Gallons Plain Syrup.
½ Pint Tincture of Lemon Peel.

Mix all together, and it is ready for immediate use.

ESSENCE OF ARRACK PUNCH.

5 Gallons Strong Brandy.
3 Gallons Plain Syrup.
½ Pint Tincture of Lemon Peel.
½ Pint Tincture of Orange Peel.
3 Ounces Tincture of Allspice.
½ Wineglass Tincture of Cloves.

Mix the tinctures with the Brandy, and add the syrup.

ESSENCE OF BRANDY PUNCH.

PUNCHES

ESSENCE OF CLARET PUNCH.

5 Gallons Claret.
2½ Gallons Spirits.
3 Gallons Plain Syrup.
1 Pint Tincture of Lemon Peel.
½ Pint Raspberry Juice.
1 Ounce Tartaric Acid.
1½ Ounces Tincture of Cloves.
1½ Ounces Tincture of Cinnamon.

First dissolve the Tartaric Acid in a small portion of the Spirits. Mix the tinctures with the remainder of the Spirits. Pour the two mixtures together, and add the remaining ingredients.

CUPS

GIN PUNCH FOR BOTTLING.

Following General Ford's plans, as already described, for making sherbet, add good Gin, in the proper proportions before prescribed ; this, bottled and kept in a cool cellar or cistern, will be found an economical and excellent summer drink.

CUPS.

Use small Glass Jug.
1 Liqueur Glass Maraschino.
1 Liqueur Glass Curaçao.
1 Liqueur Glass Brandy.
1 Quart Cider.
4 Lumps of Ice.
  Add 1 Split of Soda Water.
Stir gently and decorate with slices of fruit in season.

CIDER CUP
(No. 1.)
(4 persons).

Use Large Glass Jug.
1 Liqueur Glass Calvados.
1 Liqueur Glass Brandy.
1 Liqueur Glass Orange Curaçao.
3 Lumps of Ice.
1 Bottle Cider.
1 Split of Soda Water.
Decorate with slice of fruit, and add 2 sprigs of mint on top.

CIDER CUP
(No. 2.)
(4 persons).

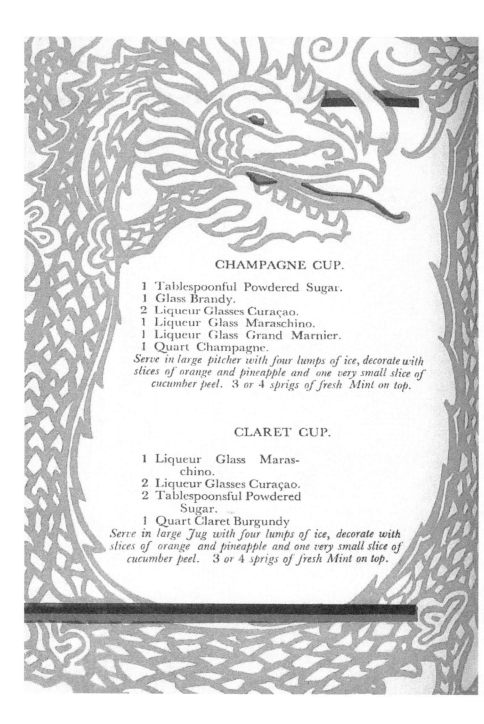

CHAMPAGNE CUP.

1 Tablespoonful Powdered Sugar.
1 Glass Brandy.
2 Liqueur Glasses Curaçao.
1 Liqueur Glass Maraschino.
1 Liqueur Glass Grand Marnier.
1 Quart Champagne.

Serve in large pitcher with four lumps of ice, decorate with slices of orange and pineapple and one very small slice of cucumber peel. 3 or 4 sprigs of fresh Mint on top.

CLARET CUP.

1 Liqueur Glass Maraschino.
2 Liqueur Glasses Curaçao.
2 Tablespoonsful Powdered Sugar.
1 Quart Claret Burgundy

Serve in large Jug with four lumps of ice, decorate with slices of orange and pineapple and one very small slice of cucumber peel. 3 or 4 sprigs of fresh Mint on top.

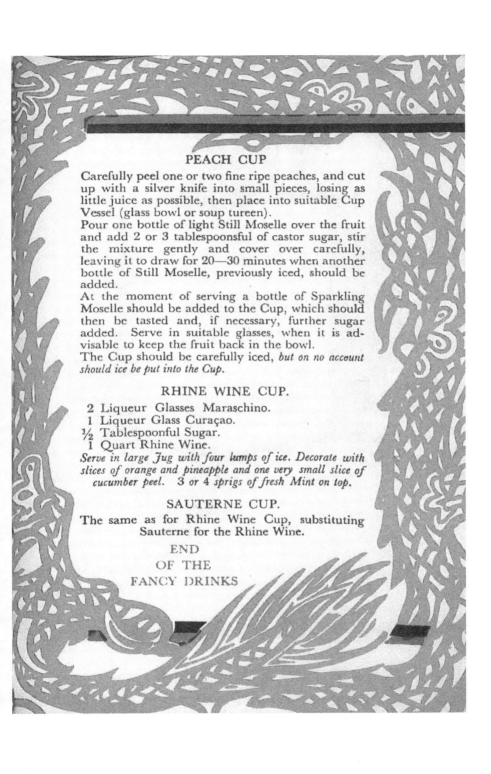

PEACH CUP

Carefully peel one or two fine ripe peaches, and cut up with a silver knife into small pieces, losing as little juice as possible, then place into suitable Cup Vessel (glass bowl or soup tureen).

Pour one bottle of light Still Moselle over the fruit and add 2 or 3 tablespoonsful of castor sugar, stir the mixture gently and cover over carefully, leaving it to draw for 20—30 minutes when another bottle of Still Moselle, previously iced, should be added.

At the moment of serving a bottle of Sparkling Moselle should be added to the Cup, which should then be tasted and, if necessary, further sugar added. Serve in suitable glasses, when it is advisable to keep the fruit back in the bowl.

The Cup should be carefully iced, *but on no account should ice be put into the Cup.*

RHINE WINE CUP.

2 Liqueur Glasses Maraschino.
1 Liqueur Glass Curaçao.
½ Tablespoonful Sugar.
1 Quart Rhine Wine.

Serve in large Jug with four lumps of ice. Decorate with slices of orange and pineapple and one very small slice of cucumber peel. 3 or 4 sprigs of fresh Mint on top.

SAUTERNE CUP.

The same as for Rhine Wine Cup, substituting Sauterne for the Rhine Wine.

END
OF THE
FANCY DRINKS

THE LUCKY HOUR OF GREAT WINES.

By " COLETTE."

I was very well brought up. As convincing proof of such a categorical assertion, let me say that when I was barely three years of age my father, who believed in gentle and progressive methods, gave me a full liqueur glass of a reddish-brown wine sent to him from his native Southern France ; the Muscat Wine of Frontignan.

It was like a sun-stroke, or love at first sight, or the sudden realization of a nervous system ; this consecration rendered me a worthy disciple of Wine for ever afterwards. A little later, I learnt to quaff my glass of mulled wine, aromatic with cinnamon and lemon, to a dinner of boiled chestnuts. At the age when one can barely read I was spelling out, drop by drop, red Burgundies, old and light, and dazzling Yquems. Champagne passed in its turn, a murmur of foam, leaping pearls of air, across birthday dinners and first communion festivities : with it came grey Puisaye truffles. . . . A fine lesson from which I acquired familiar and discreet knowledge of wine, not swallowed greedily, but measured out into narrow glasses, absorbed in mouthfuls with long spaces in between, and carefully reflected upon.

It was between my eleventh and my fifteenth years that this beautiful educational programme was completed. My mother feared that, as I grew older, I should become anæmic. One by one, she unearthed from their dry sand some bottles which were ageing beneath our house in a cellar—it is, thank Heavens ! still intact—carved out of the granite itself. Whenever I think about it, I envy the little brat who was so privileged. To accompany my modest provisions on my return to school—a cutlet, the drumstick of a chicken, or one of those hard cheeses that are matured beneath wood-cinders and which one breaks into splinters with a blow from one's fist like a pane of glass—I had Château-Larose, Château-Lafite, Chambertin and Corton which had escaped the Prussians in 1870. Certain of the wines had perished, and were pale and smelt faintly of dead roses ; they rested in a bed of tannin which dyed the bottles deeply ; but most of them kept their fine fire, strength and vigour. What delightful times those were ! I drained the cream of the paternal cellar, glass by glass, delicately . . . . My mother recorked the opened bottles and contemplated the glory of the French vintages on my colouring cheeks.

How lucky are the children who do not distend their stomachs with great draughts of artificially reddened wine at meals ! How well advised are the parents who dole out to their offspring an inch of pure wine—meaning " pure " in the highest sense of the word—and teach them that : " When it is not meal-time, you have the pump, the tap, the springs and filters. Water is for thirst. Wine is, according to its quality and its flavour, a necessary tonic, a luxury or a tribute paid to food."

Is it not also nourishment ? What lovely times those were when the natives of my village in Lower Burgundy would gather around a bottle clad in dust and silky cobwebs and kiss their fingers in the air to it, exclaiming—even before tasting it—" Nectar ! " Do you not admit, then, that in telling you about wine here I am speaking about what I know ? It is not a

little thing to have learnt contempt, at an early age, both for those who drink no wine and those who drink too much.

The Vineyard and Wine are great mysteries. Alone in the vegetable kingdom, the vine gives us a true understanding of the savour of the earth. And how faithfully it is translated! It partakes of, and reveals, all the secrets of the soil. Through it we realise that even flint can be living, yielding, nourishing. Even the unemotional chalk weeps, in wine, golden tears. If you transplant a vine to a distant country, it struggles to retain its personality and sometimes triumphs over powerful mineral chemicals. Gathered near Algiers, the white wines remember perfectly, for many years, the noble Bordeaux scion which sweetened them just sufficiently, softened them and gave them gaiety. It is Madeira that colours and warms the heavy dry wine which ripens at Château-Chalon, on the ridge of a narrow rocky plateau.

From the grapes flourishing on the twisted vine-plant, heavy, of a transparent dull agate colour, or blue and powdered with silver, the eye falls to the bare wood, like a wooden snake, wedged in between two boulders; with what, then, does this southern land feed itself, where there is no rain and which is only kept together by a network of roots? The dews of the night and the sunshine of the day are enough for it—the fire of a star, the life-sweat of another star—marvels.

What single cloudless day, what soft late rainfall decide that a vintage shall be great among the others?

Human care can do almost nothing towards it ; it is all celestial wizardry, the orbits of planets, sunspots.

Follow with your finger, my fair readers, on the map, beneath the eye of Nectar, the honours-list of the " years." Learn your vintage chronology and the litanies of Saints Estèphe, Julien, Emilion . . . Fashion would have it so. If—still in the name of Fashion—you do not eat enough, at any rate you have lately learnt how to drink. You lack discernment and preference, and in this these charts will help you. It is sweet, merely by uttering the names of our provinces and our towns, to sing the praises of the venerated vineyards. It is profitable both to the mind and to the body—believe me—to taste wine in its home, in the country which gave it all it possesses. What surprises has not a carefully thought out pilgrimage in store for you ! Young wine, tried in the dim light of the wine-cellar—virgin Angevin wine, uncorked beneath a dusty bower beside a high road on a stormy summer afternoon—or exciting, odds and ends discovered in an old cellar which either does not know its wealth or has forgotten it . . . . From such a cellar, in Franche-Comté, I once fled as though I had robbed a museum . . . . Some crazy furniture, sold by auction in a little village square, included, between the dressing table, an iron bedstead and some empty bottles, six full bottles ; it was there that I made, whilst yet a young girl, the acquaintance of a Prince, fiery, imperious and treacherous as are all great seducers : Jurançon. These six bottles made me more interested in their country of origin than any professor could have done. I admit that at such a price geography lessons are not at everyone's beck and call. And we drank this glorious wine, one day, in the low-ceilinged parlour of an inn, so dark that we never even knew the colour of the wine. Its memory is like that which a lady traveller retains of a nocturnal adventure, of the Unknown whose face she does not see, and who reveals himself only in his kisses.

Gastronomic snobbishness has given rise to a collection of Inns, such as never used to be seen. It reverences Wine. Will wisdom be reborn of an ill-enlightened faith, confessed by mouths armour-plated by a hundred cocktails, poisonous aperitifs, withering spirits ? Let us hope so. With the dawn of old age I can offer, for my small part, the example of a stomach that has no remorse or damage, a friendly liver and a sensitive palate, preserved by honest wine. Fill then, Nectar, this glass which I hold out to you. A fine and simple wine as you yourself love it, you who know, giving a light bubble in which play the ruddy fires of a great Burgundian ancestor, the topaz of Yquem, the balas ruby, sometimes tinged with mauve, of violet-perfumed Bordeaux. . . .

And may your slim chef of a bronzed cellarer understand me when I clink your dainty glass against a thick-sided goblet ; you know well—there comes a time in life when one worships youth—that on a southern shore there is being kept for me a chapelet of wickered demi-johns. One vintage fills them, the next finds them empty and fills them in its turn. Do not disdain, you who lay down fine bottles, these short-lived wines ; they are clear, dry, varied, they flow evenly from the throat to the paunch and do not tarry on their way. So long as the temperament of the wine be warm, we do not care, down there, if the day be sultry, but drink great draughts of that wine which refreshes us and leaves behind it a double taste of muscat and of cedar-wood.

[*For permission to reprint the above article in English we are indebted to the courtesy of Madame Colette, who wrote it, and of the Maison Nicolas, to whom its copyright belongs.*]

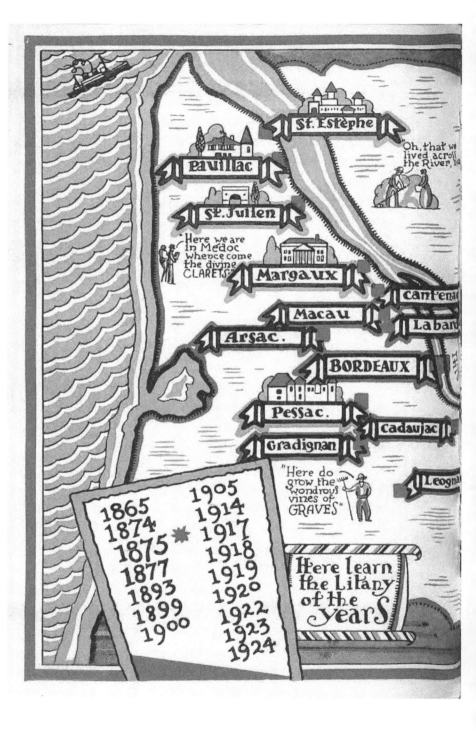

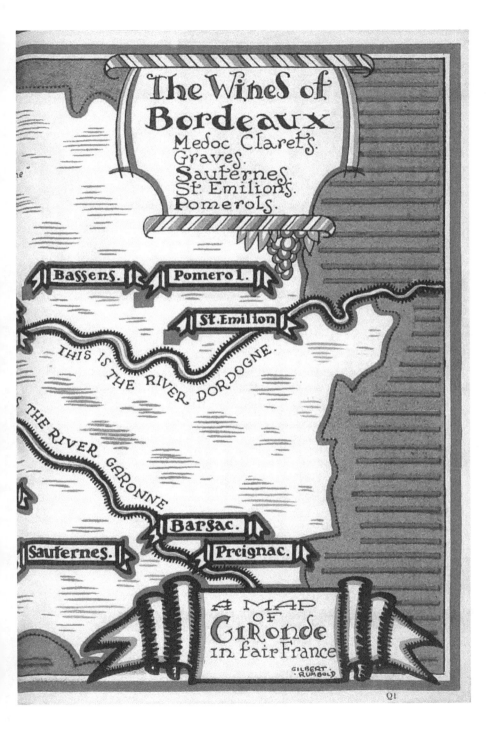

The Wines of Bordeaux

At the head of a glorious list of the still wines of France undoubtedly must stand the beatific Growths that come out of the 'departement' of the Gironde, where the old city of Bordeaux wields her sceptre. Thence come the magnificent 'Classed Growths' of the Médoc Clarets, beloved of the connoisseur, the Vins de Graves, red and white, the Sauternes, the St. Emilions, and the especial Pomerols. We will deal with each of these in turn, that you may know something of their individual characteristics, and of their classifications.

BORDEAUX

THE CLASSED CLARETS.

Among the great wines produced throughout the world, with the possible exception of Champagnes, the ' Classed Growths' of the Médoc Clarets stand alone, particularly those bearing upon their labels the ' hall mark '—" Mis en bouteilles au Château," or, as we say, Château-Bottled.

Before, therefore, proceeding with the actual description of the various ' Growths,' it will be as well to pause here to enquire into the exact meaning of this highly important phrase, so that we may see just why such labelling is held in respect by the Claret connoisseur.

We must go back to a very important landmark in the history of the great Clarets, to the year 1846, when the practice of ' Château Bottling ' was first inaugurated. Until that year, the famous Châteaux of the Gironde disposed of their vintage to the big dealers in bulk, and the bottling of the wine was, in consequence, entirely in the hands of the trade. In that year, however, the celebrated Château Lafite obtained the very special privilege of bottling the vintage, or at least part of it, actually upon the estate. It will be seen at once that in this way the wine was definitely authenticated, and the ' mark ' became, in consequence, highly prized. During the years that followed, other Châteaux adopted the practice, until to-day quite a number of the ' elect ' are permitted to carry on the privileged practice of ' Château Bottling.' These, then, are the wines so highly esteemed, that stand above all others of the Gironde, the very names of which come smoothly and lusciously off the tongue of the connoisseur.

BORDEAUX

These sixty-two red wines of the Haut-Médoc, the great Clarets, are classed into Five 'Growths' or Sections—" First Growths," " Second Growths," etc., a classification which has been in use since 1855, when it was drawn up by a committee of experts. This classification may be accepted as representing the 'bigness' and power of the wines in a descending scale of alcoholic content. It does not follow that a Fourth and Fifth Growth is inferior in quality to wines in higher classes, as no more delicate refined wines exist than many of the Fourth and Fifth Growths.

With the exception of Château Haut-Brion, nearly all the famous red wines of France are grown in the Haut-Médoc.

There are five supremely important communes in the Médoc—Pauillac, Cantenac, Margaux, Saint-Julien and Saint-Estèphe—famous in all Christian countries. There are five less important ones, Saint-Laurent, Labarde, Ludon, Arsac and Macau. These ten communes contain all the sixty-two *Crûs Classés*.

FIRST GROWTHS.

The four Giants among Clarets.

Château.	Commune.
CHÂTEAU LAFITE.	PAUILLAC.
CHÂTEAU MARGAUX.	MARGAUX.
CHÂTEAU LATOUR.	PAUILLAC.
CHÂTEAU HAUT-BRION.	PESSAC.

BORDEAUX

SECOND GROWTHS.

Château.	Commune.
MOUTON-ROTHSCHILD.	PAUILLAC.
RAUSAN-SÉGLA.	MARGAUX.
RAUZAN-GASSIES.	MARGAUX.
LÉOVILLE-LASCASES.	ST. JULIEN.
LÉOVILLE-POYFERRE.	ST. JULIEN.
LÉOVILLE-BARTON.	ST. JULIEN.
DURFORT-VIVENS.	MARGAUX.
LASCOMBES.	MARGAUX.
GRUAUD-LAROSE-FAURE.	ST. JULIEN.
GRUAUD-LAROSE-SARGET.	ST. JULIEN.
BRANE-CANTENAC.	CANTENAC.
PICHON-LONGUEVILLE.	PAUILLAC.
PICHON-LALANDE.	PAUILLAC.
DUCRU-BEAUCAILLOU.	ST. JULIEN.
COS D'ESTOURNEL.	ST. ESTÈPHE.
MONTROSE.	ST. ESTÈPHE.

THIRD GROWTHS.

Château.	Commune.
KIRWAN.	CANTENAC.
D'ISSAN.	CANTENAC.
LAGRANCE.	ST. JULIEN.
LANGOA.	ST. JULIEN.
GISCOURS.	LABARDE.
BROWN-CANTENAC.	CANTENAC.
MALESCOT-ST.-EXUPÉRY.	MARGAUX.
PALMER.	MARGAUX.
LA LAGUNE.	LUDON.
DESMIRAIL.	MARGAUX.
CALON-SÉGUR.	ST. ESTÈPHE.
FERRIÈRE.	MARGAUX.
MARQUIS-D'ALESME-BECKER.	MARGAUX.

BORDEAUX

FOURTH GROWTHS

Château.	Commune.
ST.-PIERRE-BONTEMPS.	ST. JULIEN.
ST.-PIERRE-SEVAISTRE.	ST. JULIEN.
BRANAIRE-DUCRU.	ST. JULIEN.
TALBOT.	ST. JULIEN.
DUHART-MILON.	PAUILLAC.
POUJET.	CANTENAC.
LATOUR-CARNET.	ST. LAURENT.
ROCHET.	ST. ESTÈPHE.
BEYCHEVILLE.	ST. JULIEN.
LE PRIEURÉ.	CANTENAC.
MARQUIS-DE-TERME.	MARGAUX.

FIFTH GROWTHS.

Château.	Commune.
PONTET-CANET.	PAUILLAC.
BATAILLEY.	PAUILLAC.
GRAND-PUY-LACOSTE.	PAUILLAC.
GRAND-PUY-DUCASSE.	PAUILLAC.
LYNCH-BAGES.	PAUILLAC.
LYNCH-MOUSSAS.	PAUILLAC.
DAUZAC.	LABARDE.
MOUTON-D'ARMAILHACQ.	PAUILLAC.
DU TERTE.	ARSAC.
HAUT-BAGES.	PAUILLAC.
PÉDESCLAUX.	PAUILLAC.
BELGRAVE.	ST. LAURENT.
CAMENSAC.	ST. LAURENT.
COS-LABORY.	ST. ESTÈPHE.
CLERC-MILON.	PAUILLAC.
CROIZET-BAGES.	PAUILLAC.
CANREMERLE.	MACAU.

BORDEAUX

THE OUTSTANDING VINTAGES OF CLARET FOR THE LAST 60 YEARS AND THEIR CHIEF CHARACTERISTICS ARE :—

1865. A wonderful vintage.

1870. Big. Hard for many years, but now sought for by connoisseurs.

1874. Good.

1875. Probably the best vintage ever made in the Haut-Médoc ; the wines are now becoming a little worn, but are still most interesting. A few are still to be found in certain wine lists.

1877. Good.

1893. Excellent.

1899. A wonderful vintage. The best since 1875. Full, round, splendid bouquet, with all the highest qualities of the wines of the Haut-Médoc.

1900. Excellent wines : sweeter than, but not so much body as, 1899's. A wonderful vintage.

1905. Good wines, sweet and fine bouquet.

1914. Good, sound wines, possessing fine colour, good body and roundness of flavour. A very good vintage resembling the celebrated vintage of 1900.

1917. This is a good vintage. The wines possess smoothness, delicacy and breeding. Their chief characteristic is their agreeableness. They are reasonable in price.

1918. A good vintage that has much improved, clean, with good body and softness of texture.

1919. Very good, healthy, and attractive, good body.

1920. Has developed well, good breed, élégance, finesse and splendid body. It has lost its original hardness.

1922. A plentiful and fairly good year.

1923. A good year.

1924. An excellent vintage, some of the higher classed wines likely to become very fine.

235

HERE ARE THE "GIANTS" AMONG THE MEDOC CLARETS

THE FOUR FIRST CLASSED GROWTHS.

CHÂTEAU LAFITE.

Of exquisite bouquet and rich full flavour. The first 'Château Bottled' Lafite goes back to the year 1846.

CHÂTEAU MARGAUX.

The most delicate of these fair wines with a unique and individual flavour, sometimes compared with the faint perfume of cedar wood. A beautiful, smooth wine that strikes softly on the palate. The true Château Margaux must not be confused with the many other wines, some of them of high classification, which are produced in the Commune of Margaux. The finest vintages are to be found among the years 1899, 1900, 1904, 1911, 1914, 1917, 1918 and 1920. Château Margaux was first Château Bottled in 1847.

CHÂTEAU LATOUR.

A magnificent wine of wonderful fragrance and particularly noted for its peculiarly delicate body. This is a very safe wine to lay down, for its body develops in bottle, and lasts for many years. The golden years of Château Latour are as follows :—
1858, 1862, 1864, 1865, 1868, 1869, 1870, 1875, 1877, 1878, and in more recent times 1920 is outstanding.

CHÂTEAU HAUT-BRION.

A wine distinguished by its beautiful colour, exquisite bouquet, and very fine flavour. It is interesting to note that all Château bottlings at Haut-Brion, previous to the year 1900, were delivered to the 'trade' unlabelled. Vintages subsequent to this date bear the Château mark on corks and capsules, but the label shown below did not appear until 1904, since which all bottles are so distinguished.

BORDEAUX

THE RED GRAVES.

The vineyard district to the South of Bordeaux, that is known as Graves, produces a vast quantity of really excellent wine, both red and white, the former being predominant, at least in quantity. In order, therefore, to prevent confusion in our purpose, it must be explained that the White Graves are usually 'classed' (in a similar way to the Médoc Clarets) among the Classification of the White Wines, and will therefore be dealt with under that heading. For the moment we are only concerned with the Red Graves, and here is appended a list of selected growths, representing the best among a large number of marks.

En passant, it should be noted that in no circumstances should the Graves be confused with the Sauternes. They usually appear in wine lists together under the general heading of White Bordeaux.

BORDEAUX

THE RED GRAVES

Château.	Commune.
LA MISSION-HAUT-BRION.	PESSAC.
PAPE CLEMENT.	PESSAC.
CAMPONAC (1st Growth)	PESSAC.
BON-AIR (1st Growth)	MERIGNAC.
DE MOULERENS.	GRADIGNAN.
DE LAURENZANE.	GRADIGNAN.
HAUT-BAILLY.	LÉOGNAN.
OLIVIER (1st Growth)	LÉOGNAN.
DU BOUSCAUT.	CADAUJAC.
LARRIVET-HAUT-BRION.	LÉOGNAN.
DE CHEVALIER	LÉOGNAN.
CARBONNIEUX.	LÉOGNAN.
SMITH-HAUT-LAFITTE.	MARTILLAC.

BORDEAUX

OF SAINT-EMILION.

The Commune of Saint-Emilion is famed the whole world over for the production of the luscious red wines bearing its name. Since the year 1889 estate-bottling has become almost universal among the *Premiers Crus* of Saint-Emilion, with a splendid increase in public confidence and demand as a direct result. Château Ausone, for example, is a worthy competitor of the four first growths of the Médoc, and frequently fetches a higher price than they do, ranking as "Premier des Grands Crûs de Saint-Emilion."

The Clarets of Saint-Emilion are of a distinctive type. They are quite different from the wines of the Médoc and Graves districts, and they are also entirely different from the wines of Burgundy, with which they are sometimes mistakenly compared. They are the highest expression of the "vins de côtes." They have body, beautiful colour and an agreeable bouquet. The best wines of Saint-Emilion are of a rich, dark-red colour. It is said to be one of the qualities of the "bon vin de Saint-Emilion" to untie the tongue and loosen speech—*le vin parle et fait parler.*

The following are noteworthy growths :—

Château.	Château.
AUSONE.	BELAIRE.
MAGDELAINE.	BEAUSÉJOUR.
CANON LA GAFFELIÉRE.	FONPLÉGADE.
	LE CURÉ BON.

BORDEAUX

Chateau.	Chateau.
PAVIE.	VILLEMAURINE
BALEAU.	L'ARROSÉE.
BERLIQUET.	LA CLUSIÈRE.
COUTET.	GRAND-PONTET.
TROIS-MOULINS.	FRANC-MAYNE.
BELLEVUE.	LA GAFFELIÈRE-NAUDES.
PETIT FAURIE DE SOUTHARD.	DOMAINE DE GRAND-FAURIE.
PALAT-SAINT-GEORGES.	CLOS DES JACOBINS.
JEAN DU MAYNE.	CLOS FOURTET.
CLOS HAUT-SIMARD.	FIGEAC.
CHEVAL-BLANC.	

OF POMEROL.

Among the great wines the beautiful red produced from the Pomerol district more than deserve the fame they have enjoyed through the years. All the best Pomerols possess good body, and a truly magnificent bouquet, a happy ensemble due to the exceptional qualities of the soil on which the vines flourish. The Pomerols are especially famed for what is known as the ' bouquet de la truffe.'

Here are some of the best Growths :—
CHÂTEAU PETRUS.
CHÂTEAU TROTANOY.
CHÂTEAU NENIN.
CHÂTEAU LACABANNE.
CHÂTEAU MOULIN-À-VENT DE LAVAU.
CHÂTEAU DE SALES.
CHÂTEAU ROUSSILLON.

BORDEAUX

THE CLASSED WHITE WINES.

From the districts of SAUTERNES and BARSAC come the finest white wines produced in the Gironde. As with the famous Médoc Clarets, they are classed into numbered "Growths," and the practice of Château Bottling is carried on in the same way among the very best marks.

A great quantity of excellent white wine is obtained from the Graves vineyards, but the output of red wine from that district is considerably greater.

The Sauternes district, on the contrary, is famous *solely on account of its wonderful luscious white wines.*

BORDEAUX

Unlike the Médoc wines, which come from eleven different communes, the great white wines come from five communes only, namely :—SAUTERNES, BARSAC, BOMMES, PREIGNAC and FARGUES. Although the soil in these districts is peculiarly suitable to the best production of white wines, it is interesting to note that another factor enters into the wine-making here. For the best wines, the white grapes of Sauternes are used from at least two and sometimes three different species of vines, and the grapes are not considered sufficiently ripe to be gathered until they appear wrinkled and over-ripe. The grape must have a thin layer of " mustiness," called *pourriture*, before it is picked. This undoubtedly has much to do with the eventual fine flavour of the wines.

Here is a list of the finest Growths :—

BORDEAUX

GRAND FIRST GROWTH.

Château.   Commune.

YQUEM.   SAUTERNES.

FIRST GROWTHS.

LA TOUR BLANCHE.	BOMMES.
PEYRAGUEY.	BOMMES.
LAFAUFIE-PEYRAGUEY.	BOMMES.
DE RAYNE-VIGNEAU.	BOMMES.
DE SUDUIRAUT	PREIGNAC.
COUTET.	BARSAC.
CLIMENS.	BARSAC.
GUIRAUD.	SAUTERNES.
RIEUSSAC.	FARGUES.
RABAUD-PROMIS.	BOMMES.
SIGALAS-RABAUD.	BOMMES.

SECOND GROWTHS.

DE MYRAT.	BARSAC.
DOISY.	BARSAC.
D'ARCHE.	SAUTERNES.
FILHOT	SAUTERNES.
BROUSTET-NÉRAC.	BARSAC.
CAILLOU.	BARSAC.
SUAU.	BARSAC.
DE MALLE.	PREIGNAC.
LAMOTHE.	SAUTERNES.
LA MONTAGNE.	PREIGNAC.

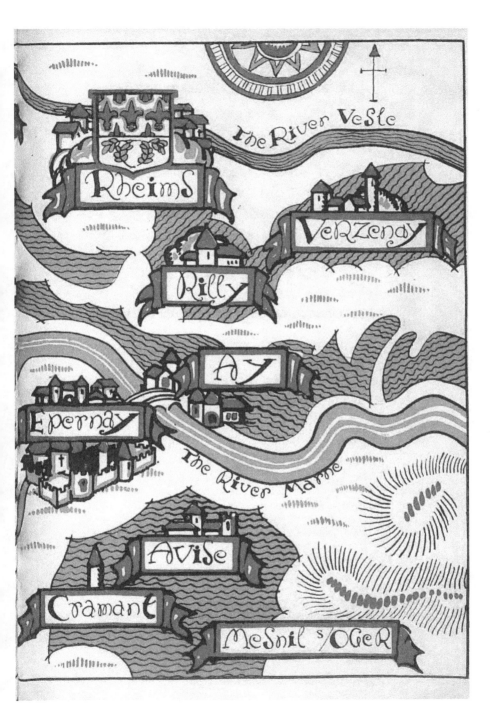

CHAMPAGNE

"King Charles! King Charles!"

Singularly fitting would it seem that the 'Merrie Monarch' should be the figure responsible for the introduction of the sparkling, light, elegant, and expensive Wine of Champagne into England. Surrounded by a Court, the richness and elegance of which was famed throughout Europe, he searched for a 'Wine of Fashion' that should express to a nicety the regal luxury, the gaiety, and the sparkling wit of his time. He found it all in Champagne.*

---

* To Lord Chesterfield, who always imported his own wine from France, is attributed this toast, which might well have been welcome in that Court :
  "Give me Champaign, and fill it to the brim,
  I'll toast in bumpers ev'ry lovely Limb!"

CHAMPAGNE

From which it must not be assumed that the history of Champagne began in that austere epoch. Indeed, its glorious history goes right back to at least the First Century A.D., when it is recorded that the great Roman Empire, jealous of the 'good Gallic wines,' decreed that the famous vines of Rheims be dug up, and replaced with corn. Just two hundred years later, the Roman soldiers themselves replanted the vineyards, since when they thrived and prospered exceedingly until the coming of the year 1914, when the shells of the enemy and the trenches of the Allies turned the precious vineyards once more into a desolate waste. The Great War, combined with the coincident pestilence of a tiny insect called Phylloxera, caused the greatest crisis ever experienced in the Champagne industry. Unfortunately, the comparatively small area from which the whole of the world's Champagne is produced became, by a vicious twist of Fortune's Wheel, a strategic point in the great battleground, and many a famous vineyard was seared by the ugly scar of a trench. The task of re-planting the vines was therefore a colossal one which had to be faced by the great growers at the close of hostilities. That they have succeeded, that once more the regal and time-honoured names are taking their proper places at the head of post-war vintages, is a tremendous tribute to the tenacity and purposefulness of the French character. To understand this fully, it should be explained that the very special quality of Champagne is in considerable measure due to a judicious blending of the produce of several particular vines, vines which require an incredible amount of care and attention in actual growth, as well as considerable time for their proper fruition.

CHAMPAGNE

It was the Master-Cellarer of the Abbey of Hautvillers, Dom Pérignon by name, who first introduced, in the XVIIth Century, this practice of combining the grapes of various vineyards, and a peculiar method of producing the luscious froth and at the same time clarifying the wine, in the actual bottle. Last, but by no means least, he introduced the use of the cork stopper for bottling wines. His methods, with certain improvements, have been in use ever since.

If, now, we would learn something of Champagne, it is first necessary to realise that although true Champagne is only permitted to be produced within a certain strict confine in the district surrounding Rheims, it does not follow that all the vineyards within that province are producers of Champagne. Champagne is a wine of such exacting properties that only a limited number of vineyards in the area are considered to possess the necessary soil, geographical position, exposure to sunlight, etc., to bear grapes of the very particular quality required for perfect blending. The great reputation of Champagne rests to a large extent upon this factor, and in consequence the strictest laws are in force to cover it.

Before we can learn to judge Champagne properly, it is essential to know how it is made, a process, in its main principles, not at all difficult to understand. It has already been explained how the grapes from various vineyards are brought together for careful blending. That is the first stage, at vintage time, usually towards the end of September.

Each batch of fresh grapes is pressed in special large-surface presses, peculiar to the Champagne district,

CHAMPAGNE

and particular care is taken to prevent the red colouring matter of the skin from 'staining' the wine. Only the first pressings are used to make the best wine. The mass of crushed grapes remaining on the pan of the press (and from which the first juice has been extracted) are then re-pressed, and a juice known as 'deuxièmes tailles' is obtained. It is from the 'deuxièmes tailles' that the cheap Champagnes are produced.

The first juice is known as 'must' and this is run into huge vats, where it remains and settles for at least two days. It is then barrelled, clear and free from rough sediment. Now commences the natural fermentation of the 'must,' the sugar contained in it being converted into alcohol and carbonic acid gas, and a further sediment, called 'lees' begins to settle. By December, the low temperature normally stops the fermentation, and it is here that an early cold snap, or a late winter, are extremes that must have considerable effect upon the quality of the eventual wine. As a matter of fact, the statement " eventual " wine is perhaps not too accurate, as there are quite a few people who consider Champagne very palatable at this particular stage. When one speaks of "Natural" Champagne, one refers to the wine at this period of its preparation. This " Natural " Champagne must eventually possess a sediment, as the fermentation is not yet complete, and the return of warmer weather will lead to a re-commencement of this process.

The bulk of the produce, however, is carried several stages further before finally reaching the outer world and its lucky consumer.

CHAMPAGNE

Towards the end of April most of the wine is bottled, the balance being placed on reserve in the spacious underground cellars of the shipper. Now it is important to note that at this time the wine is placed into the actual bottles that will subsequently be so elegantly 'dressed,' and in which the Champagne is eventually sold. The clarifying and re-fermentation processes which follow are all carried out while the wine is in the bottle. These bottles are so made that they will withstand the considerable pressure to which they have to be subjected which may amount to as much as 7 or 8 atmospheres, and the inside of the glass must be absolutely smooth to prevent any possibility of sediment adhering to it.

The bottle having been filled, it is now firmly stoppered with a special cork, known as the 'drawing cork.' This, be it noted, is *not* the eventual 'shipping cork' which we know so well, but of this more anon. The next important step is to collect the sediment as it is generated, so that it may be removed from the bottle, and leave the wine crystal clear. This is done by placing the bottles upon special racks, known as 'desks.' At first the bottles recline cork downwards in the racks at an angle of 50 to 60 degrees, and every day, over a considerable period, each bottle is given a peculiar jerk and rotation, leaving it each time a little nearer the

CHAMPAGNE

vertical. The object of this, of course, is to get all the sediment to settle upon the cork, and finally, when the bottles have actually reached the vertical position, a condition known as 'finished on end,' they are ready for the 'dégorgement,' or extraction of the sediment coated cork. Refrigeration has been largely adopted for this purpose, the wine in the neck of the bottle being frozen solid, thus permitting the easy extraction of the cork, to which the deposit is adhering, without a drop of the wine being spilt.

Now comes the operation called 'dosing.' This consists in the adding of a special liquor of pure cane sugar-candy dissolved in high quality wines, and it is the addition of this liquor in varying proportions that gives to the wine the qualifications " Extra Dry," " Drapeau Américain," " Dry," " Demi-Sec " or " Goût Français " (sweet).

Now the bottle is ready to be stoppered with the 'shipping cork' with which it is eventually sold. Many people have been puzzled to find a comparatively new cork, upon opening a good branded Champagne that they have been assured is a very old wine. From the foregoing it will be seen how such a circumstance might come about. It merely means that the wine has not been 'cleared' until shortly before its sale, as very frequently occurs. Whilst touching upon this question of corking, it must be

CHAMPAGNE

mentioned that a Champagne cork should always be in actual contact with the Wine, so that when storing the bottle must always be placed upon its side.

Having now learnt something of the particular manner in which Champagne is produced, let us discover how we can be absolutely certain that the wine we buy is really genuine. This is necessary on account of the fact that many attempts have been made from time to time to market wines which one might be led to assume are legitimate Champagnes, whereas in actual fact they are sparkling wines, possibly prepared in the same manner as true Champagne, but outside the recognised Champagne district. It must be explained that French law is particularly strict on this point, even to the extent of insisting that no Champagne Wine can be exported from the Rheims district *in barrel* without losing its legal right to the name "Champagne." As a consequence the only wine in the world which can rightly claim the appellation "Champagne" is that actually bottled in the legal Champagne district, from grapes gathered within that same confines. Every bottle containing genuine Champagne wine must further bear the word "Champagne" upon the label in large type, and also upon that portion of the cork which is inside the neck of the bottle. As has already been mentioned, attempts have been made by many producers of sparkling wines to get round these precise requirements, by using upon their labels such terms as "Vins Champagnisés." By an act of 1927, the use of this particular phrase was made illegal.

Unfortunately the peculiar shape and ' dressing ' of a Champagne bottle is not protected in any way by law, so that this provides an easy means for the unscrupulous imitator.

Another even more subtle form of imitation is that sometimes practised by manufacturers whose

CHAMPAGNE

wines are made actually in the recognised Champagne district.

Their labels usually bear the name of a town well known as being in the area, but unless the word ' Champagne ' appears on label and cork the wine can in no way be accepted as genuine.

The classical Vintage years of Champagne during the past fifty years are 1874, 1884, 1889, 1892, 1893, 1900, 1904, 1906, 1911, 1913, 1919, 1920, 1921.

HERE ARE THE NAMES OF THE GREAT CHAMPAGNE SHIPPERS, under which the wines are sold.

AYALA & CIE., *AY.*
BINET (VEUVE), FILS ET CIE., *RHEIMS.*
BOLLINGER, J., *AY.*
CLIQUOT-PONSARDIN (VEUVE), *RHEIMS.*
DELBECK ET CIE., *RHEIMS.*
DE ST. MARCEAUX, *RHEIMS.*
DEUTZ & GELDERMANN, *AY.*
DUMINY ET CIE., *AY.*
GOULET (VEUVE) GEORGE ET CIE., *RHEIMS.*
HEIDSIECK ET CIE. (MONOPOLE AND DRY
    MONOPOLE), *RHEIMS.*
HEIDSIECK, CHARLES, *RHEIMS.*
IRROY, E. ET CIE., *RHEIMS.*
KRUG ET CIE., *RHEIMS.*
LANSON, J., *RILLY-LA-MONTAGE,* and *RHEIMS.*
MOËT & CHANDON, *EPERNAY.*
MONTEBELLO (DUC DE), *MARENIL-SUR-AY.*
MUMM (G. H.), *RHEIMS.*
PERRIER-JOUET ET CIE., *EPERNAY.*
PIPER-HEIDSIECK, *RHEIMS.*
POL ROGER ET CIE., *EPERNAY.*
POMMERY & GRENO, *RHEIMS.*
ROEDERER, LOUIS, *RHEIMS.*
RUINART, PÈRE ET FILS, *RHEIMS.*

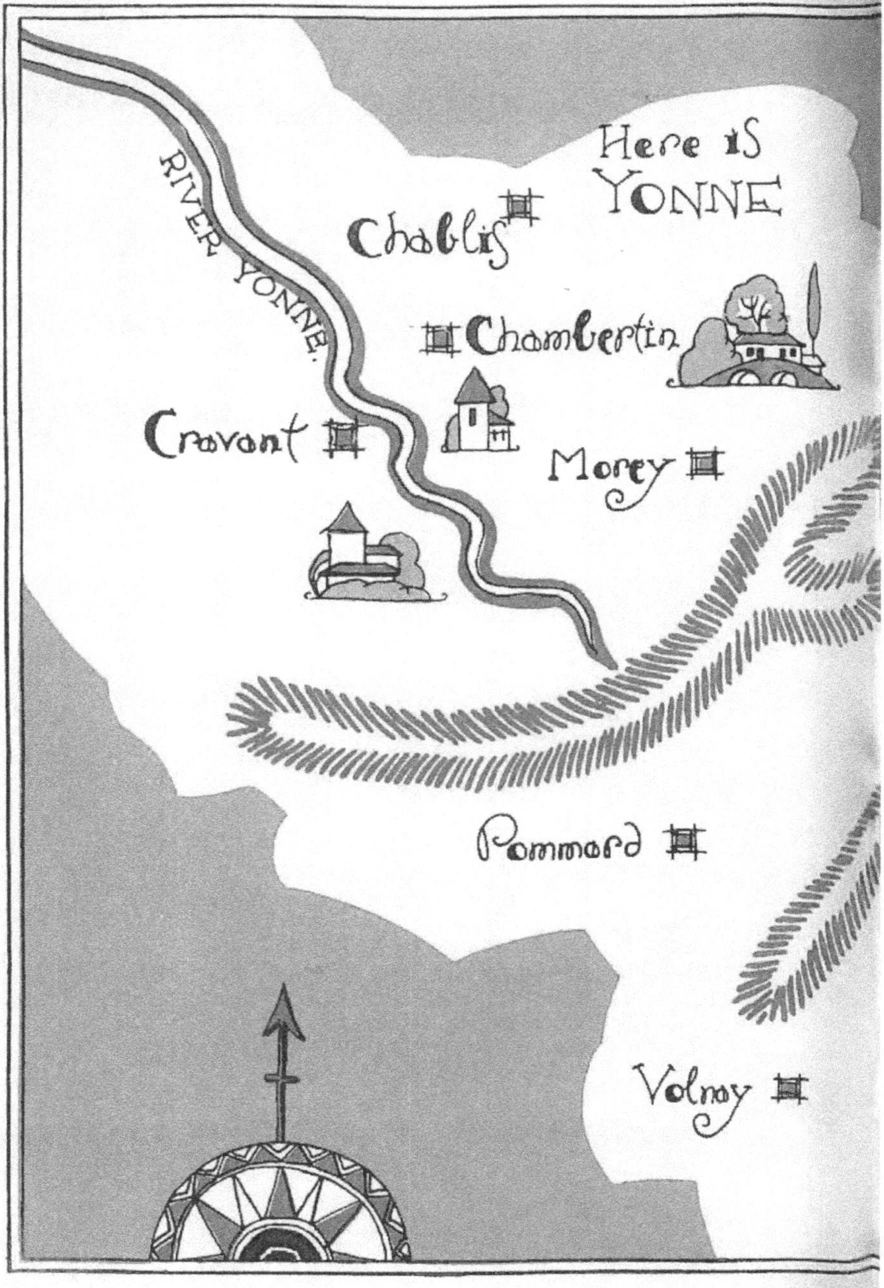

Here is YONNE
Chablis
RIVER YONNE.
Chambertin
Cravant
Morey
Pommard
Volnay

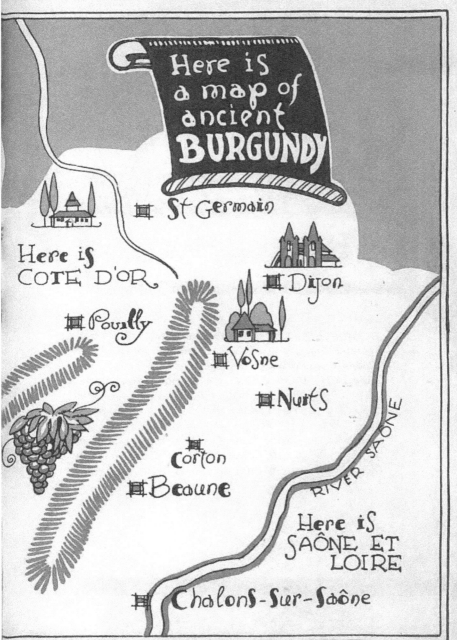

BURGUNDY

In the good year fifteen hundred and twelve splendid King, Louis XII of France found it politic (and, we would like to think, pleasurable) to send to King James IV of Scotland a present. An especial present. A gift, indeed, that should completely befit an occasion so regal and so gallant. It is not particularly surprising, therefore, to learn that in these circumstances King Louis ordered a great painted ship to be filled with puncheons of delicious wine from the province of old Burgundy, and in despatching it

BURGUNDY

North of the Tweed, introduced the famous Burgundian blood of the grape into the British Isles for the first time.

Since that great occasion the vintages of Burgundy have established for themselves a reputation throughout the whole civilised world second only perhaps to the Champagnes. The old province of Burgundy itself passed into a memory through the shambles of the French Revolution, but its glorious vines live on. Take a look at the map of France. Over towards her Eastern boundary you will find five 'departements' that bear the following names :— Côte D'Or, Saone-et-Loire, Yonne, Ain and Aube. It is from these districts, particularly the former, that the magnificent red and white wines called Burgundies are produced. No wine produced outside

BURGUNDY

their boundaries can properly be called Burgundies, although the law is certainly not so stringent upon this point as in the case of the Champagnes. True Burgundy, like Champagne, is the produce of certain particular vines, grown upon a particular soil, and under specific conditions which are only to be found in the districts named above. On the other hand, real Burgundy is marketed in such a manner that it is very much more difficult to obtain assurance of accurate origin than is the case with either Champagne or Claret. For example, in purchasing a Château Bottled Claret one can he absolutely certain that the wine is the careful and perfect product of the vineyard of the actual Château. In the case of Burgundy these conditions are fundamentally different, for a single great vineyard bearing a famous name and situated, perhaps in a commune of equal fame, may be split up among as many as a dozen owners and vintagers, each producing wine in their own fashion, and possessing their own brand labels, etc. Even so, the wine is eventually sold under the name of the whole vineyard, and this fact renders it necessary for the connoisseur to exercise extreme care in selecting a Burgundy that will be consistent with his exact tastes.

The Côte D'Or, first among the Burgundy producing ' departements,' is renowned for its Red

BURGUNDY

wines, most of the better known white wines coming from the Yonne, with the town of Chablis as its centre. For the purpose of classification the Côte D'Or is divided into two districts, the first known as the Côte de Nuits, and the second as the Côte de Beaune. From the Côte de Nuits come the marvellous Chambertin, quite a giant among the Red Burgundies, the Romanée-Conti, and the Clos de Vougeot. The Côte de Beaune produces such fine wines as Corton, Clos du Roi, Les Renardes, and, of course, Beaune itself.

The ' departement ' of Saone-et-Loire is principally famed for the wines of Mâcon (red) and those of Pouilly (white).

One important point worthy of note is that true Burgundy should never show any tendency to sweetness. If the wine displays this ' taint ' it may usually be assumed that cane sugar has been added at some time, possibly by the maker, in order to render a decidedly mediocré wine palatable to the untrained taste. Burgundy should always be of a soft and delicate flavour, without sweetness, and, on the other hand, without being really dry or ' tart ', and should possess a bouquet not quite so insistent as, shall we say, Claret.

BURGUNDY

RED BURGUNDIES.

There is no official classification of Red Burgundy, but the following list gives the best of the growths:

CHAMBERTIN.
CLOS DE VOUGEOT.
LES MUSIGNY.
CLOS SAINT-JACQUES.
ROMANÉE-CONTI.
VOLNAY.
CORTON.
MÂCON.
LES GRANDS ESCHEZEAUX.
NUITS-PREMEAUX.
CHABLIS.
BEAUNE.
LES RICHEBOURGS.
LES ARVELETS.
NUITS SAINT-GEORGES.
CLOS DE TART.
BONNES MARES.
POMMARD.
SAVIGNY.
ROMANÉE LA TACHE.
SAVIGNY.

BURGUNDY

CHABLIS.

The leading brokers classify White Burgundies as follows:

1st Growths.

VANDÉSIR.	LES CLOS.
VALMUR.	GRENOUILLE.
BLANCHOT.	LES PREUSES.
BOUGROS.	

2nd Growths.

CHAPELOT.	CHATAIN.
MONTÉE DE TONNERRE.	MONTMAIN. BEUGNON.
MONT DE MILIEU.	LES FORÊTS. LES LYS.
VAILLON.	LES EPINOTTES.
FOURCHAUME.	VAULORENT.
SÉCHET.	

3rd Growths.

PARGUES.	BUTEAUX.
SOYAT.	VIELLES VOIES.
VALVAN.	

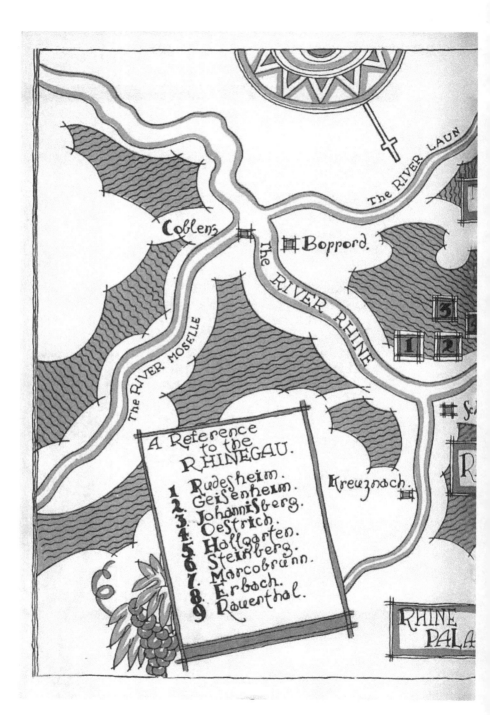

HOCKS (Rhine Wines) STEINWEINS & MOSELLES

HOCKS.

Germany cannot be said to be a prolific producer of wine, at least of wine made from the actual grapes of the Fatherland, although quite an appreciable quantity is fermented from imported grapes. Of these latter, however, we need not deal here, except only to warn the neophyte that such wines can never be considered as being up to anything like fine quality, and are therefore to be avoided. Really fine German wine is never very plentiful, but this fact may be regarded as offset to some degree by the exceedingly fine quality of what is produced—the luscious and fruity Hocks, Steinweins, and Moselles.

The term Hock is a somewhat general one, and is usually understood to mean a wine of quality originating in the districts of the Rhineland. For purposes of classification the Rhineland is split into three main districts, Rheingau, Rheinhessen, and Rheinpfalz, and each of these districts gives us a wine of individual character.

The most famous of these is the Rheingau, which occupies some twenty kilometres of the right bank of the Rhine, from Niederwald to Lorch.

HOCKS AND MOSELLES

The RHEINGAU wines are almost exclusively made from Riesling grapes, and are somewhat crisper in flavour than those originating from the other two districts. They are distinguished for their great elegance.

The Rheingau includes the famous growths of Rauenthal, Erbach, Marcobrunn, Hattenheim, Steinberg, Oestrich, Schloss Vollrads Winkel, Schloss Johannisberg, Geisenheim and Rudesheim, the wines of which are noted for their raciness and fruit.

HOCHHEIM is included in the Rheingau district and produces some excellent wines. It is generally accepted that the English generic term of Hock, used to designate all Rhein wines, is derived from the name of the town Hochheim.

RHEINHESSEN extends along the left bank of the Rhine from Worms to Bingen. The Riesling and the Oesterreicher are the two vines most cultivated in this district.

Rheinhessen wines are somewhat milder than those of the Rheingau, and show more variety than the latter. In Oppenheim full-bodied wines possessing great fruit are made; Nierstein wines are mellower, but at the same time more elegant.

The wines of Rheinhessen improve more quickly in bottle than those of the Rheingau, and are, as a rule, deeper in colour.

HOCKS AND MOSELLES

RHEINPFALZ. Wines originating from the Rheinpfalz, which is the largest wine-producing district in Germany, are familiarly known to Englishmen as Palatinate wines.

The Rheinpfalz enjoys an extraordinarily mild climate, and in the Mittelhaardt district, between Neustadt and Duerkheim, where the vines are grown close to the ground in order to obtain as much heat as possible from the earth as well as from the sun, the finest wines are produced.

The best known growths come from the districts of Ungstein, Duerkheim, Wachenheim, Forst, Deidesheim and Ruppertsberg.

The " Auslese " wines from all these districts, made from grapes specially selected for their ripeness, are remarkable for their fruit, bouquet, and great body.

The " Trockenbeeren-Auslese " wines are made from grapes that have almost reached the raisin stage (hence the word " Trockenbeeren," *i.e.*, " Dry Berries "), and are therefore very highly concentrated, possessing a great deal of fruit and natural sweetness.

Other terms indicating that wines have been made from selected grapes, such as " Edelbeeren-Auslese," " Edelgewaechs," " Spaetlese," mean that the grapes have been allowed to hang on the vines longer after the vintage gathering in order to take advantage of fine, sunny Autumn days.

HOCKS AND MOSELLES

MOSELLES.

The wines of the MOSELLE and its tributaries, the SAAR and the RUWER, are remarkable for their delicate perfume and subtle flavour due to a great extent to the silicious nature of the soil upon which the Riesling vine thrives so well.

They may be called the ideal luncheon wines owing to their comparatively low alcoholic strength and their pleasing natural dryness. From a medical point of view they can be strongly recommended, as they are quickly assimilated and therefore easily digested.

The finest growths of the Moselle proper are to be found on either bank of the river. To name but a few districts in alphabetical order : Berncastel-Cues, Brauneberg, Dhron, Enkirch, Erden, Graach, Josefshof, Lieser, Piesport, Reil, Uerzig, Wehlen and Zeltingen.

The names of the different vineyards are added to that of the district under such tempting titles as " Himmelreich "—Kingdom of Heaven ; " Rosenberg "—Garden of Roses ; " Goldtröpfchen "— Drops of Gold ; " Wurzgarten "—Garden of Spices.

HOCKS AND MOSELLES

STEINWEIN.

STEINWEIN is grown in the vineyards round about Wurzburg.

Since the Middle Ages it has always been bottled in the famous squat Frankish flagons called " Bocksbeutel."

It is a wine of great elegance and rare bouquet with quite a surprising amount of body and flavour in spite of its pale colour.

1921 HOCKS AND MOSELLES.

A magnificent vintage, considered the best for a generation or more. Particularly the Hocks. The wines are very full, round, and vinous. The Hocks have great keeping properties.

Here is a list of the finest German Wines :

RHINE WINES :

FROM RHEINGAU.

RAUENTHAL.
ERBACH.
MARCOBRUNN.
HATTENHEIM.
STEINBERG CABINET.
OESTRICHER EISERBERG.
SCHLOSS VOLLRADS WINKEL.
SCHLOSS JOHANNISBERG.
GEISENHEIM.
RUDESHEIM BERG.
HOCHHEIM NEUBERG.

HOCKS AND MOSELLES

FROM RHEINHESSEN.

SCHARLACHBERG.
NIERSTEIN.
OPPENHEIM.
LAUBENHEIM.
BODENHEIM.

FROM RHEINPFALZ (PALATINATE).

RUPERTSBERG AUSLESE.
DEIDESHEIM.
FORST.
UNGSTEIN.
DURKHEIM.

STEINWEIN.

WURZBURGER NEUBERG.

MOSELLES.

ZEITINGER.
BRAUNEBERGER.
BERNCASTELER.
WILTINGEN KUPP.
PIESPORTER KIRCHEL.
ZELTINGER SCHLOSSBERG.
ZELTINGER SONNENUHR.
OBEREMMELER HERRENBERG.
ERDENER TREPPCHEN AUSLESE.
SCHARZHOFBERGER.

PORT

Port has a peculiar and romantic interest for all English-speaking people, since for over a hundred years, from the middle of the eighteenth until well past the middle of the nineteenth centuries, it was not only the best known wine in England, but it was the only wine that many highly conservative people would allow to appear upon their tables. It came, indeed, to be regarded, with Roast Beef, as being symbolic of English domestic life. There is a story told of a Warwickshire squire who, shortly after Queen Victoria's Coronation, found that a son of his had secretly introduced some bottles of Claret into the house. The squire, his face distorted with fury and contempt, impounded the bottles and poured their contents down the nearest convenient pig-sty, apostrophizing his son thus whilst doing so : "How dare ye bring these new-fangled foreign wines into my house ? Good honest English Port was good enough for my father and my grandfather, and it shall be good enough for my son ! "

Which shows that a little ignorance is often a blessing in disguise.

PORT

Port is still the most generally popular wine in England, and it is the only wine (even Sherry not excepted) that you may always be certain of finding wherever a British Inn Sign swings. Naturally it varies very much in quality, but it is always sure to be genuine Port, as it is a very serious offence to sell a wine as Port unless it satisfies the definition of being a "fortified wine produced in the region of the Douro Valley and exported through the bar of Oporto." At the same time there is considerable difference between the beverage you will obtain by signifying assent to the question, " Port, me lord ? " huskily whispered by the butler at a dinner-party in Carlton House Terrace, and what you get by falling in with the suggestion, " What about a glass of Port Wine, dearie ? " in the Private Bar of "Ye Olde Duck and Chinaman," round the corner.

Port, as we know it now, is produced by the judicious blending of various wines whose process of fermentation is then retarded by the addition of a small quantity of Brandy, which causes it to mature very slowly and to become mellow with age. The final product falls under one of three headings, depending upon the way in which it is matured. It is either Vintage Port, or Tawny Port, or Ruby Port.

PORT

Vintage Port is the wine of one particular year, and is only produced when the wines of that year are particularly fine. All Vintage Ports have a peculiar character of their own, and the true Port connoisseur can tell at a sip to what particular year a Vintage Port belongs. It is bottled two, and sometimes three, years after the vintage and matures entirely in bottle.

Tawny Port, so called from its lighter colour, is a blend of the wine of several years, and is matured entirely in casks. It does not possess the richness or the bouquet of Vintage Port, and is, as a rule, made from wines which, although good, are not sufficiently excellent to stand alone.

Ruby Ports are something between the two. They are matured partly in cask and partly in bottle. They are very popular with Port lovers who cannot afford the high prices which Vintage Ports now fetch. A really good Ruby Port may even at times deceive an expert, but it cannot be relied upon, and varies from bottle to bottle.

Port is shipped under the names of the Blenders. Most of the old-established shippers have English names, thus bearing witness to the fact that a hundred years ago Port was in very truth an English wine, manufactured in Portugal by the English and for the English.

The best Port Vintages of the past forty years were 1890, 1896, 1900, 1908, 1912, 1917 and 1919, and the principal Oporto Shippers, under whose names the Vintage Ports are sold, are :

PORT

BUTLER, NEPHEW & CO.
COCKBURN, SMITHIES & CO.
CROFT & CO.
DELAFORCE, SONS & CO.
DIXON.
DOW (SILVA & COUSENS).
FERREIRA BROS.
FEUERHEERD BROS. & CO., LTD.
FONSECA & CO. (GUIMARAENS & CO.).
GONZALEZ, BYASS & CO.
GOULD, CAMPBELL & CO.
GRAHAM, WM. & JOHN, & CO.
HUNT, ROOPE & CO.
MACKENZIE & CO., LTD.
MORGAN BROS.
OFFLEY FORRESTER, LTD.
REBELLO VALENTE (ROBERTSON BROS. &
    CO., AND G. SIMON & WHELON).
SANDEMAN & CO.
SMITH, WOODHOUSE & CO., LTD.
TAIT, STORMOUTH & CO.
TAYLOR, FLADGATE & YEATMAN.
VAN ZELLERS & CO.
WARRE & CO.

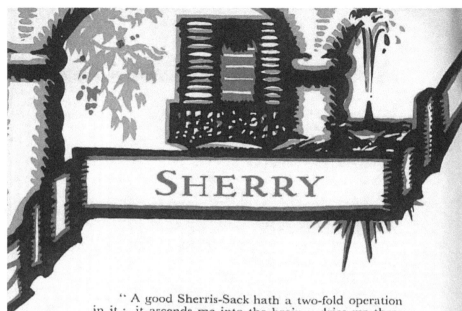

SHERRY

"A good Sherris-Sack hath a two-fold operation in it; it ascends me into the brain; dries me there all the foolish, and dull, and crudy vapours which environ it, makes it apprehensive, quick, inventive, full of nimble, fiery and delectable shape, which delivered o'er to the voice which is the birth, becomes excellent wit. The second property of your excellent Sherris is the warming of the blood; which before cold and settled left the liver white and pale, which is the badge of pusillanimity and cowardice; but the Sherris warms it, and makes it course from the inwards to the parts extreme"—Thus spoke Shakes-

SHERRY

peare, through the lips of the robust Falstaff, and who will deny that he spoke from the heart? For the immortal Bard, akin to many great men of his time, was truly appreciative of the subtle vapours of ' Sherris-Sack," or Sherry, as we have since learned to call it in an age when brevity is counted among the seven virtues. Yet, curiously enough, even " Sherris-Sack ' is a derivation, possessing an origin in ' Jerez-Sec '—Jerez being the name of the Spanish province from which this special wine has always been produced. Nowadays, of course, we are prone to include Madeira. Sherry, good Sherry, still remains among the first loves on the palate of the connoisseur, although, perhaps, its more general popularity is not now so great as it was fifty years ago. The direct reason for this lies in the fact that from one cause or another Sherries that were scarcely deserving of the name were from time to time foisted upon a market slow in discovering that ignorance is not always bliss. Be careful, therefore, in acquiring your Sherry, if you would enjoy its real delights as you should.

SHERRY

It must always be remembered that fine Sherry is as much the product of the expert blender as of the grower, and for this reason the shipper's name on the bottle is of considerable importance. That name must be one with a reputation behind it if you are to be quite sure of your ground.

The qualities of Sherry fall naturally into three main categories. The first is known as *Fino*, a delicate wine of pale colour and gentle fragrance. The second is called *Amontillado*, a heavier wine which demands a longer time to mellow and acquire its distinctive character and fuller flavour. The third is classed as *Oloroso*, and is a much darker and heavier wine than the others. Now, of course, each of these main classes cover many degrees and varieties of excellence. Thus we find the famous Vino de Pasto falls into the *Fino* classification, while Amoroso, or old Golden Sherry and the Brown Sherries are members of the last class. A great feature of the finest Sherry is the fact that, not only does it continue to improve with age, but its fine qualities are not impaired by being left uncorked. A decanter of Sherry may therefore be relied upon over an indefinite period, even if left unstoppered.

SHERRY

Here is a list of shippers whose products can always be relied upon when their names appear on the labels.

WILLIAMS & HUMBERT.	JEREZ.
V. DIAZ & CO.	PORT ST. MARY.
GONZALEZ, BYASS & CO., LTD.	JEREZ.
MARTINEZ, GASSIOT & CO., LTD.	PORT ST. MARY.
ANTONIO R. RUIZ Y HERMANOS.	JEREZ.
DUFF, GORDON & CO.	PORT ST. MARY.
GARVEY & CO.	JEREZ.
MACKENZIE & CO., LTD.	JEREZ.
MANUEL MISA.	JEREZ.
PEDRO DOMECQ.	JEREZ.

THE END
OF THE
WINES

CONCLUDING REMARKS ABOUT SPECIAL OCCASIONS.

In the pages of this book we have endeavoured to give, as succinctly as possible, a compendium of drinks of all kinds, and we only hope that it will be found useful by those who are wise enough to secure a copy before the Censor gets upon its track. There is little to add. We may mention that all the characters in the book are real persons, and that everything we have said about them is true, in substance and in fact.

There is, however, one last word of advice which we feel bound to offer to you, one which is in some sort in the nature of a word of warning ; and that is to be particularly careful not to produce the wrong kind of drinks for the great occasions of your life. When, for instance, your tailor pays you a formal call with a view to obtaining a reduction of the amount of your credit with him, you will not appease him by offering to split a bottle of Champagne with him, pleading the ghastliness of your poverty the while. And never offer ginger-beer to the lady whose favour you intend to curry, however honourably, before the evening is out. Port should rarely be served at breakfast, and it is not correct to offer a parting guest a cocktail, unless you feel that you have given him such a bad dinner that he is probably going on to have another one somewhere else, and needs an appetizer.

Many books have been written on the subject of what wines should be served with different foods, but the best and only real guide is the individual experience of each one of us. Remember always that there are certain people who cannot drink Burgundy, others that cannot bear Champagne or Port. It is always safest to ask your guests what they would like to drink. If they say they do not mind, it means that they want Champagne ; if they prefer any other kind of wine they will say so ; the psychology of this is quite clear ; Champagne is always expensive, so there is a natural reticence about demanding it outright ; other wines are actually probably more expensive, but they *can* be cheaper, and there is therefore no hesitation in suggesting them.

Wine is a solace and a consolation, and it has been given to man for his happiness. To deny oneself the pleasure of Vintage is to declare oneself to be a pessimist and a Kill-Joy. If this book should, by any mischance, fall into the hands of such an one, we can only hope that he will peruse it earnestly, with the end that when he has finished it he will take a cab to the Savoy Hotel, and will penetrate reverently into that sanctum where Harry Craddock plies the Art which is the main theme upon which this book, has been conceived. For without the ingenuity, knowledge and skill of Harry Craddock it could never have seen the light of day.

ADDITIONAL COCKTAILS

BACARDI COCKTAIL.

¼ Lemon Juice or Lime Juice.
¼ Grenadine.
½ Bacardi Rum.
Shake well and strain into cocktail glass.

BAMBOO COCKTAIL.

¼ French Vermouth.
¼ Italian Vermouth.
½ Dry Sherry.
Stir well and strain into cocktail glass.

BLACKTHORN COCKTAIL (No. 2.)

Dash Orange Bitters.
⅓ Italian Vermouth.
⅔ Sloe Gin
Stir well and strain into cocktail glass.

BOOKSELLERS' (SPECIAL) PRIDE.

¼ Orange Juice.
¼ Calvados.
½ Gin—Booth's Dry.
A green cherry that has been macerated in orange Curaçao.
Shake well and strain into cocktail glass, afterwards adding the green cherry.

DEVONSHIRE PRIDE.

1 Dash Lemon Juice.
⅓ Swedish Punch.
⅔ Calvados (Apple Brandy).
Shake well and strain into cocktail glass.

ADDITIONAL COCKTAILS

1 Dash Grenadine.
1/4 Orange Juice.
1/4 Pricota (Apricot Brandy).
1/4 Calvados (Apple Brandy).
1/4 Gin—Booth's Dry.
*Shake well and strain into cock-
tail glass.*

**GOLDEN
DAWN.**

2 Dashes Absinthe.
1/3 Hercules.
2/3 Gin—Booth's Dry.
*Shake well and strain into cock-
tail glass.*

GUN COTTON.

1 Dash Angostura Bitters.
1/4 Italian Vermouth.
1/4 Calvados (Apple Brandy).
1/2 Brandy.
*Shake well and strain into cock-
tail glass.*

**JERSEY
LIGHTNING.**

1/4 Lemon Juice.
1/4 Orange Juice.
1/2 Cointreau.
*Shake well and strain into cock-
tail glass.*

**LULU'S
FAVOURITE.**

Printed in the USA
CPSIA information can be obtained
at www.ICGtesting.com
LVHW091656211223
767102LV00001B/145